Byblos

Beyrout

LEBANON

ANTIL...

Damascus

GOLAN
HEIGHTS

MEDITERRANEAN

SEA

Acre

Caphernaum

Haifa

Tiberias

SEA OF GALILEE

Cana

Nazareth

Beth She'an
(Beisan)

East Ghor Canal

Jerash

Samaria

Jordan River

Succoth

Tel Aviv

Amman

Jaffa

Mt. Gerizim

Qasr el Azraq

HISHAM'S PALACE

Lydda

Jericho ×

Qasr al Amra

GETHSEMANE

△ Mt. Nebo

Qasr al Mashatta

Jerusalem ×

Bethabara

Bethlehem

Madaba

Hebron

DEAD
SEA

Wadi el Mujib

Karak

N E G E V

D E S E R T

Mt. Hor △

Beidha

Petra

Wadi Musa

Maan

S I N A I

E N I N S U L A

Guweira

0   10   20   30   40   50 MILES

0 10 20 30 40 50 KILOMETERS

Rumm

The Holy Land—from the Valley of the Kings at Thebes to Petra in the Jordanian desert, to the stones of Jerusalem and the faces of Beyrout—these are some of the splendors explored in Robert Payne's new book. Following the *Splendors* of France, Greece and Israel, Mr. Payne writes here of his experiences in traveling through Egypt, Jordan, Israel and Lebanon.

The temples in the Nile Valley still remind us of the Pharaohs, of Tutankhamen the boy-king and Queen Hatshepsut, who were worshiped as gods in ancient Egypt. Hours—and worlds— away in Cairo the Caliphs left monuments of their own to the vast empire of Egyptian Islam. And near a church outside Cairo stands "the Virgin's Tree," according to Coptic legend the site where the holy family rested during the flight from Israel.

In the Hashemite Kingdom of Jordan the nature-worshiping spirit of Lawrence of Arabia hovers over the Wadi Rumm, and we recall that King David attacked the city of Ammon (Amman), though he was helped by a later king of that city in his war against Absalom. Along the Jordan Valley the reader travels with Mr. Payne and discovers the magical beauty of the rose-red Nabataean city of Petra, Crusader fortresses, and Mount Hor, where Aaron was buried according to the command given to Moses.

The Dead Sea and the River Jordan are heavy with reminders of the Old Testament and the Gospels. On their banks Arabs ply their trade, as from time immemorial, in souvenirs of the holy sites. In Jerusalem itself, holy to Jews, Christians and Moslems, time "is still Biblical time." The Holy Sepulchre, the Western Wall and the Dome of the Rock all have their pilgrims who even today are drawn to worship the rocks and stones of Jerusalem, as was the author. In Hebron we visit the Tomb of Abraham, and on Mount Gerizim the High Priest of the Samaritans.

In the Lebanon that Mr. Payne saw, there were temples at Baalbek and Phoenician ruins in Byblos. Visiting Beyrout, he was told by a Lebanese, "We survive as a result of a series of miracles."

Miracles, ancient and modern-day, are daily fare in the Holy Land, and readers of this book will finish it with a sense of having been there and seen it for themselves, with a sense of recognition and perhaps new insights for those who have already been, and with increased anticipation for those who hope to go.

Born in Cornwall, England, ROBERT PAYNE has lived, traveled and studied in England, France, South Africa and China. He has been a shipwright, an armaments officer, a professor of English, a translator and a correspondent. His books include *The Holy Sword, The Holy Fire, The Gold of Troy* and *The Life and Death of Adolf Hitler.*

THE SPLENDOR OF THE HOLY LAND

A CassCanfield BOOK

Books by Robert Payne

THE SPLENDOR OF

HARPER & ROW, PUBLISHERS
New York, Hagerstown, San Francisco,
London

THE HOLY LAND

EGYPT
JORDAN
ISRAEL
LEBANON

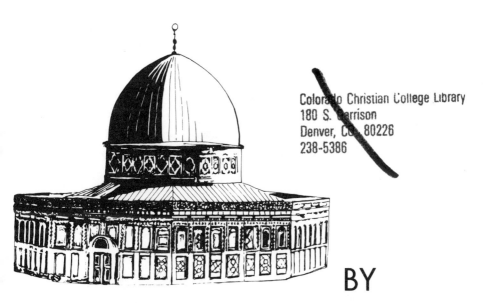

BY
ROBERT PAYNE

FIRST EDITION

Designed by Gloria Adelson

Library of Congress Cataloging in Publication Data

Payne, Pierre Stephen Robert, 1911–
  The splendor of the Holy Land—Egypt, Jordan, Israel, Lebanon.
    (A Cass Canfield Book)
    Includes index.
    1. Egypt—Description and travel—1945–
2. Jordan—Description and travel. 3. Israel—
Description and travel. 4. Lebanon—Description and travel. I. Title.
DS49.7.P33 1976   915.69′04   76–5523
ISBN 0–06–013294–9

---

76 77 78 79 80 81 10 9 8 7 6 5 4 3 2 1

For MIREILLE and STEVE

CONTENTS

ILLUSTRATIONS

THE TRAVELER IN THE HOLY LAND

We are all travelers now, though we no longer seem to know why we are traveling. We fly to the legendary places as though we were taking a train to the suburbs, and nothing surprises us any more. Tahiti is a day's journey from New York, and Timbuktu is even closer. Ormuz and Mozambique and Samarkand, all those places anchored in childhood's dreams, are within reach, and soon enough we shall be spending our weekends in Antarctica. The Golden Age is upon us; we are permitted to pay later and to enjoy our travels without opening our purses. Airplanes, like flying whales, carry their huge cargoes of passengers packed uncomfortably together like sardines across the vast oceans, while the travel posters announce that there is scarcely anywhere in the world where you cannot spend a perpetual summer afternoon among the yellow sands—

> *How from that Saphire Fount the crisped Brooks,*
> *Rowling in Orient Pearl and sands of Gold,*
> *With mazie error under pendant shades*
> *Ran Nectar . . .*

Milton's imagination, rowling in Orient Pearl, found its richest food in the Holy Land. He had one advantage over his modern counterpart: he had never been there, and his poetry is therefore lit with the light of imaginary suns. The trouble about the contemporary version of Paradise is that it is all too earthy, too comfortable, too attainable. There is something to be said for making the journey more arduous.

1

In the Middle Ages, when men set out on pilgrimage to Jerusalem, they sold their possessions, said farewell to their families, and counted it a miracle and a blessing if they returned alive. They walked or rode by slow stages, and there was time enough to stand and stare. Each country they passed through was like a cloak worn round their shoulders. There was the easy camaraderie of the inns and hospices, the sense of a common purpose, midnight prayers, the ringing of bells, smells of horsedung, leather and straw, and always the cold white dawns. The journey was a sacrament, and their eyes were turned to the East. For them Jerusalem was far more than the Church of the Holy Sepulchre: the city was an altar radiating power and blessedness, surrounded by many other altars of almost equal sanctity. The Mount of the Transfiguration, Galilee, Nazareth, Bethlehem, the River Jordan—there was no end to the places which God had sanctified. No doubt many men went for the sake of adventure, for fighting and loot, but most of them seem to have gone for no other purpose than to stand in the places where God had walked.

It was a time when the roads were filled with horsemen, when the priests rode as hard as the rest, and at the end of every day's journey there was a sanctuary to be visited and a prayer to be offered by dust-stained, weary men, who regarded a tankard of wine and a bowl of gruel as reward for a day's hardships. The dust of France, Italy, Dalmatia and Asia Minor entered their pores, and became a part of them. We who fly from New York to Lydda in a single hop and find ourselves half an hour later safely installed in Jerusalem—we have flown through empty air and gathered no nourishment for the journey. We have simply opened the door, found Jerusalem, and are ill-prepared.

It is not our fault, for we are creatures of our time, but most of us, I think, are aware that something is missing. Speed kills the imagination and the taste of things. I have seen men doing the Sea of Galilee, speeding round the lake at fifty miles an hour, and in half an afternoon they have seen Tiberias, Magdala, Caphernaum, Tabgha, and the Mount of the Beatitudes, thus leaving themselves with the second half of the afternoon to explore Cana, Nazareth, Sepphoris and the Mount of the Transfiguration. It can be done, and there is no law to prevent it. But in the Holy Land the camel's pace is too fast, and even the donkey's pace may be treacherous. Around the Sea of Galilee, certainly, it is best to walk slowly and there is no harm in walking barefoot.

The old travelers knew the proper spells. They knew that the better part of traveling was in standing still. They knew, too, that place is not where we are, but where others have been, and that half of place is light, and the study of light is at least as important as the study of the shapes of earth. The glow on the walls of cities is like the glow of faces. Nearly all the holy places of the earth derive some part of their beauty from the peculiar richness of their light. Jerusalem acquires its golden light from its golden stone and from the light beating up from the Judaean wilderness, and the silver radiance over the island of Delos comes from the marriage of the shining sea and the marble island. Light roars like a wave up the Theban cliffs facing Karnak, pours like a fountain over the cliffs of Delphi, swirls round Venice, drenches Isfahan like spring rains, so that everything glitters. In much the same way Peking acquires its radiance from the sands of the Gobi floating in the indigo blue sky. These are things to be savored slowly: it takes time to watch the light from morning to sunset. The best travelers walk at the pace of snails.

The buses take you from one holy site to another, and the travel director permits you to stay twenty minutes in the Church of the Holy Sepulchre so that the bus can go off to Gethsemane and Bethany. Travel director? But why should there be any travel directors at all? A traveler who obeys orders is only a half or a quarter of a traveler. Once travel was discovery, adventure, accomplishment, a fierce new light beating down on the voyager at every new prospect, every new city captured by enchanted eyes. But the enchantment is nearly over. Soon there will be no more cakes and ale, no more bedtime stories.

Nevertheless, for a few more years, we can travel in the Holy Land with a sense of its strangeness. Though we take shelter under the oak of Mamre and walk in the courts of Jerusalem, we are still strangers traveling through a legendary land, aware that we are seeing everything through the veil of legends; and this veil, instead of obstructing our vision, unaccountably makes everything brighter. The world of legends begins on the Nile and flows eastward. It is a dying world, and year by year the light of legends grows dimmer.

Sometimes, too, we shall discover that the legends scarcely live up to our expectations. In Sunday school I dreamed of Zion as a stupendous palace of gleaming towers fashioned out of glass and jewels, guarded by angels armed with many-colored spears. Today you can walk across a valley in Jerusalem and see a notice which says: ZION 200 METRES, and there is an arrow pointing in the direction of a modern church dedicated to the Dormition of the Virgin. This is not the Zion I had dreamed about while the flies droned in the Sunday school and Miss Cornwallis-West in her high-necked blouse spoke primly about our sins and the glory that would come to us if we set ourselves resolutely against them. But what was sin? We were never quite sure. In some mysterious way sin was the enemy of the palace of the angelic hosts, and if we committed a sufficient number of sins we would be debarred forever from entering the palace. It must be admitted that the modern Mount Zion has very little in common with the Mount Zion depicted in our leather-bound Bibles with their glowing color-plates.

Zion was David's city, resounding in glory, the same city where on a moonlit night—and Miss Cornwallis-West's voice shuddered a little as she recounted the story—David encountered Bathsheba in her nakedness. It was not, of course, real nakedness, but something else: perhaps a visionary nakedness, as intriguing as the vision of the wheels in *Ezekiel*, which left us all gasping. Miss Cornwallis-West made her way through the Scriptures with elaborate caution, and sometimes the blood rushed unaccountably to her cheeks. Sin and Zion: was it perhaps possible that she knew a little about sin? We wished devoutly that we could be taught by someone who was not so convinced that the blood of Jesus washed all our sins away on condition that we never committed any.

Much later, when I traveled in the Holy Land, I found neither sin nor Zion. Sin vanishes in the East. Our western devotion to guilt finds no sustenance in Semitic theologies: the saints in the Thebaid did not pray for salvation from their sins so much as pray for the vision of God. In the blinding desert where a man is alone with the Alone, God's power is manifested, just as in Galilee we become aware of God's peace. The traveler in the Holy Land need not burden himself with a European concept of sin, for he is engaged in a far more dangerous traffic. Soon enough he becomes a sorcerer, a necromancer, a magician. He raises the dead, conjures up ghosts, sees what no eyes can see, hears voices speaking thousands of years ago, and where there is only desert he finds himself in the presence of long-forgotten cities and palaces. He walks with Adam in the garden and with Ruth in the alien corn. Jerusalem is everywhere, and it is all one to him whether the Crucifixion took place on this skull-shaped rock or another, for the whole land is holy.

We can no more explain the holiness of this land than we can explain our own existence on earth. There are holy places all over the world—holy springs, holy mountains, holy valleys—and by virtue of their holiness they become the possession of all men. The Holy Land is therefore *terra irredenta*, an earth we all claim, though it belongs to others. That Jerusalem should be ruled by a mayor and a city council must always seem an impropriety, for it is easier to imagine it ruled by a confederation of archangels. Though people rule over the holy places, the real owners are the wanderers who worship at the shrines even though they stand but a few moments.

So the traveler who comes to the Holy Land finds himself in full possession of it, with title deeds going back to a remote antiquity. He may have to ask permission to enter a church or to worship at a shrine, but he is perfectly aware that he is merely paying lip-service to an absurd convention; he is asking permission to enter his own house. The roads, the blades of grass, the very air are his for the asking, and he is a citizen of every city and hamlet, every field and orchard. The keepers of the shrines are merely paid functionaries, to be placated and avoided; and though they act with a formidable sense of possession, they are no more than ghostly presences. There is an art in laying these ghosts. The traveler who forgets to learn this art does so at his peril. Like the guards who begin to shoo visitors out of museums at twenty to five when the closing time is five, they belong to the deepest chambers of Hell.

The truth is that the holy places have always been coveted by merchants as a source of revenue. Nothing is so marketable as holiness. So it has been through all ages, as the first Christians discovered when they went on pilgrimage. You may touch the holy stones, but the merchants of holiness will do their best to see that you pay a fee for the privilege. To outwit them is an act of merit and to ensure their downfall is an act of surpassing merit. The traveler has a right to his own possessions.

Geographically the Holy Land has no beginning and no ending. It resembles those mediaeval maps which show the world upside down with Jerusalem at the center and the four rivers of Paradise surrounding it, while the archangels blow their trumpets at the four corners. Legendary beasts, phoenixes and griffons, wander through the enchanted forests; they are sometimes dangerous. Murderers and thieves lurk in the dark places, and sometimes they are less dangerous, for they can be paid off in current coin. At the heart of the mystery lies something very simple and very difficult to comprehend. Holiness has been formed out of the imaginations of men, and therefore it is in history and not in history. It is where men believe it to be, and is without form or substance; and when we touch the stones, we are touching our imaginations. But here and there on the earth's surface we perceive a presence that is strangely familiar and very close to the heart. A shuddering of light, a lake, a cave, a fountain, a wall, a lonely road. And always when we go on pilgrimage, we see what we have seen before in dreams and visions.

Charles Doughty, most intrepid of travelers, wrote that anyone who has ever seen palm trees and goat hair tents is changed forever. That first glimpse of the desert is like a thrust at the heart: it is so impassive, so deathly. Time comes to an end and the legends begin. Moses, Christ and Muhammad all passed through the fires of the desert. And since the desert is a devouring sheet of flame where only the boldest survive, the first sight of the black tents kindles a kind of respect and envy for the tent-dwellers, those nomads who wander where they please, as free as the air. In fact their wanderings follow precisely prescribed tracks and the tent-dweller has little more freedom of movement than the suburbanite who takes the early morning train to the city.

Nevertheless we shall find that nearly all the holy places lie close to the desert. In the desert men have thought their purest thoughts, for here they are divested of the love of created things and are alone with themselves and with God. Here they are thrown back on all that is most elementary, final and decisive. The anchorites in the desert of the Egyptian Thebaid deliberately chose to live in uninhabitable places where no one would dare to follow them. For them the desert was a garden where holiness flowered. It was more than a place of refuge; it was the essential golden background of their lives.

History sweeps across the Holy Land and is swept away. Nabataeans, Romans, Greeks, Crusaders, Turks, the French and the British have all at various times poured over it and believed that it belonged to them. They built fortifications, collected taxes, impressed the young men into their armies, made war, and in general made life as miserable as possible for as many people as possible, and then crept away. They left few traces of themselves. They came as conquerors and proved to be nothing more than visitors.

In the following pages I have attempted to describe in the form of a travel journal some of the splendor and the havoc of the Holy Land, setting down what I saw and learned during three journeys to the Middle East. I have not touched on political problems because it seemed to me that they were adequately dealt with elsewhere. I have asked the ruined monuments to speak, and they have sometimes spoken clearly, sometimes in whispers. The book begins in the Valley of the Kings and ends on the shores of the Mediterranean among the ruins of Byblos, the city where the alphabet was invented and from where the Phoenician mariners set out to conquer the known world.

For the Holy Land is where we have our beginnings, and we go back to it always like people going back to the source.

EGYPT

THE VALLEY OF THE KINGS

The Nile at Thebes had the color of dusty emeralds under the terrible copper-colored sky. I stood in the shade, wondering how people could live in that heat and marveling at the delicate shapes of the sails of the feluccas inching their way along the river, although there was no apparent wind; and sometimes the sails rippled and fell slack, and yet mysteriously the feluccas continued to sail along the river. It was noon, the furnace door had opened, everything turned gold and yellow and white, and I wondered how people could ever have chosen to build a city in this smoking desert.

There was a time when Thebes was the greatest city in the world, its power reaching out over North Africa and vast areas of the Middle East, its splendors known to Homer who called it "the city with a hundred gates." Today nothing is left except the temples and the tombs. The luxury hotels perched above the Nile seem illusory, vanishing in the heat haze and the sand. The temples and the tombs are as permanent as anything can be, the hotels are by their very nature impermanent, things of fashion, out of date as soon as they are constructed. Once Thebes was palaces and tree-shaded streets, canals and arcades, stables, smithies, forges, gardens, towering walls cut by those hundred gates, and it was said that from each of these gates, when the Pharaoh gave the signal, two hundred armored chariots issued forth. Thebes was wealth and splendor, renowned all over the known world. Now there were only a few farmers living there, hiding in their patchwork huts in the heat of the day and emerging in the afternoon to tend the pathetic fields they cultivate along the banks of the Nile.

Why, of all the places they might have chosen, did the Pharaohs choose this particular site at the bend of the river for their capital? In the noonday sun the mountains of the western desert were harsh, crystalline, rising vertically like cliffs, flashing in the sun's rays. Deep in Africa, five hundred or more miles from the Mediterranean, the great white-walled city arose on a site that was no better than a hundred others that might have been chosen along the course of the river. Why not at the next bend of the river, or at the first cataract? Five thousand years ago Thebes was an obscure frontier post. The frontier expanded, the soldiers took power, wealth poured in from the south, and about the middle of the twenty-second century B.C. the whole of Egypt from the Mediterranean to Nubia was united under a Theban prince. The documents survive and we can trace without too much difficulty the emergence of Thebes from frontier post to imperial city. But this is only part of the story, and you have to go there to realize that the place itself, the broad valley under the magnificently sculptured cliffs, flaming ochre streaked with silver, summoned the city into existence. The very contours of the land demanded excitement, and where will you find more excitement than in a great walled and bastioned city?

So they built Thebes beside the Nile and facing the cliffs for the same reason that the Athenians built Athens near the seacoast and facing the Acropolis. The landscape imposed the city. The beauty of the place cried out to be inhabited.

Something like this must have happened, but I confess there is no logic in it. It is simply the overwhelming impression produced by a landscape that was made for giants. The giants have gone, the city has vanished, the squalid luxury hotels perch on the banks of the Nile, and ancient Thebes has become modern Luxor. In happier days the rich came to spend their winters here in the sun, but now many of the hotels have closed down, others are empty shells, and Luxor has almost lost its reason for existence. It has become a staging post for the few tourists who set out to visit nearby Karnak and the Valley of the Kings. Here you hire your guides and automobiles, arrange to be ferried across the Nile, map out an itinerary, send off postcards to favorite nephews, and curse the sun which threatens to melt the cliffs and turn the Nile into a dry river-bed.

I had flown down from Cairo in a small Russian plane filled with Russians on their way to Assuan. They sat in the front of the plane, talked

loudly in Russian, complained bitterly about the Egyptians, and sometimes sat in morose silence while they thought up new complaints. What
fools the Egyptians were! How absurd their government! It would be
much better for the country if the Russians took it over and taught the
Egyptians proper habits of work! So it went on throughout the flight,
complaint following complaint, until I could scarcely prevent myself from
telling them that I understood what they were saying. I was not the only
passenger who understood them. Solange, a young art student from Paris,
half-Russian, half-French, was drinking it all in with a look of amazement
while she pretended to be reading a newspaper. When we reached Luxor
she addressed them in her ringing Russian voice: "Gentlemen colonists,
please don't hate the Egyptians so much. They work hard and they have
done you no harm!" Suddenly they were all shouting at her, fists were
clenched, they were all standing up and preparing to throw themselves at
the enemy in their midst. Just as suddenly, at the orders of the largest and
fattest of the Russians, they sat down and pretended that nothing had
happened. Solange tripped down the steps, laughing gaily.

I saw her again a little later in the morning wandering through the dusty
streets of Luxor, searching for a travel guide and an automobile for the
journey to the Western Hills. It was already hot, and would grow hotter.
It was the wrong season of the year, there were very few visitors, and the
travel bureaus had shut up shop. Some Arab boys passed with a donkey,
and it occurred to her that we might go to the Valley of the Kings on
donkey-back, but the boys could not understand what she was saying.
What puzzled me was the silence and deathliness of Luxor, the hotels
battened down, the streets deserted except for some stray dogs, the houses
looking as though they were uninhabited or abandoned. Had we arrived
at Luxor during a plague? Something else puzzled me. Solange was very
beautiful, and such women usually have the effect of fire-bells, summoning
crowds from all directions. Her long red hair streaming down her back was
set off by a green blouse, a green pleated skirt and green sandals. She was
dressed to kill, but as she walked through the empty streets, not a single
shutter opened.

Half an hour later we found a travel guide, an old man in a red fez with
a wispy beard, gentle and unassertive, until he began to calculate the cost
of the short journey to the Western Hills—so much for the ferry, for the
automobile, for the driver, for the keeper of the tomb, for the guide, and

there were six or seven tombs, six or seven keepers, six or seven guides. It all added up to a fantastic sum. "Of course it will be cheaper if there are more of you," he said. "How many more?" "We can get six people in a car. Air-conditioned cars are more expensive. You will need an air-conditioned car, of course. Then there are surcharges—the Luxor tax, the government tax." The cost kept mounting. Solange's eyes opened wide in disbelief. "Of course you could walk. You can rent a bicycle. But the tombs are very difficult to find, and the keepers must be paid, and the guides too." Happily a small group of visitors who had come from Cairo by train suddenly appeared, and they too wanted to go to the Valley of the Kings. From an astronomical price the old man, pleased that he had eight or nine visitors at his mercy, descended to a price that was merely exorbitant. "The money must be paid now!" he exclaimed, brandishing the sheet of paper on which he had written down, like hieroglyphics, his amazing computations. "Now!" he repeated, enjoying his triumph. Soon he was taking us down to the ferry, and on the other side of the Nile there appeared, as though by magic, the two cars that would take us to the Valley of the Kings.

The ferry creaked and jerked its way across the river, and left no wake. The boatmen looked as sullen as slaves, perhaps because there were so few of us on the ferry. Clearly they were underpaid, and so were the drivers of the automobiles, who were equally sullen. "It's like going to a funeral," someone said, and so of course it was: we were attending the burial of kings. We crossed the steaming plain in what seemed to be five minutes and were soon climbing up the rocky defiles of the Western Hills. There was nothing that could conceivably be called the Valley of the Kings. There was no valley: only the stark bare foothills, massive and shapeless, with the thin defiles between them, gold and yellow in the blinding sunlight. There was a small restaurant with a Coca-Cola stand, perched half way up the rocks. Here the driver stopped, explaining that after our long drive we were in need of refreshments. Here, if we waited long enough, the guides and the tomb-keepers would come to meet us. Solange was a blaze of indignation. She wanted to go to the tombs now, at once, at this very moment. The driver gazed at her pityingly. "There are rules and regulations," he said, and went off to drink Coca-Cola in a corner. It appeared that the rules and regulations involved a reassessment of fees for entering the tombs and tips for nearly everyone in sight.

It was a bad beginning, but we comforted ourselves with the thought that the guides were on their way. There were twenty-seven royal tombs in the Valley of the Kings, seven were open to the public, and we decided that only one, the tomb of Tutankhamen, needed to be examined. It was the only tomb which still contained the body of a king in a golden sarcophagus. When five guides came to the restaurant accompanied by five tomb-keepers, we issued our ultimatum. We would see Tutankhamen, and nothing else. Why? Because our money was running out. Four guides and four tomb-keepers scowled; one guide and one tomb-keeper smiled. Also, we said we had waited long enough in a restaurant we had not wanted to visit, and wanted to leave now, at once, at this very moment. Tutankhamen's tomb was opposite the restaurant. The smiling tomb-keeper announced that he would immediately go in search of the keys. We groaned. "Ah, I forgot," he said. "I have the keys with me!" The art of frustration, as practiced by tomb-keepers, is very venerable; he would have kept us another twenty minutes if we had not revolted. Solange, the arch-revolutionary, was standing outside the restaurant, twirling her blue and white patterned parasol, purring like a kitten. She had won her victory.

In this way we came out of the blinding heat into the coolness of the winding gallery brilliantly painted with ancient Egyptian gods and goddesses and inscriptions from the *Book of the Dead.* The gallery led to the tomb chamber, a small brightly lit room just large enough to contain the sarcophagus and a small platform from which we could look down at Tutankhamen in his youthful glory, encased in solid gold, superb in the insolence of death. He was about eighteen when he died, or more probably was killed in the course of a court intrigue. He was boyish still in his lifelike golden mask. His arms were folded over his golden chest, and his hands held the crook and the flail, the emblems of kingship. From his brow rose a hooded cobra and a vulture's head, also emblems of kingship. He wore a plaited beard, also of gold, and his eyes were gold, set with dark stones. This is the third and last of the gold coffins that enclosed him, the two others being in Cairo, and it is also the simplest, as though, being closer to his flesh, it was necessarily made with a greater refinement, a greater vitality. Here he is boy as well as king. The gold sheet, stamped with his image, gleams; the powerful gold hands clasp the gold crook and the gold flail; and the goldsmiths who fashioned this image have wonderfully succeeded in conveying the portrait of a youth who is sleeping and will soon awake.

The Egyptians very wisely decided that his mummified body should remain here in the shaft carved out of the living rock. He alone remains, for the other Pharaohs can be seen in the Egyptian Museum in Cairo, set side by side in a room like a mortuary, their features still recognizable, but pitted and ravaged by the centuries. I confess I prefer it this way. Ages will pass; the very site of Tutankhamen's tomb will be forgotten; sand and rockfalls will fill up the passageways; and the king will continue to sleep his long sleep, inviolable until the end of time.

Just as we were leaving Solange pointed with her parasol at the wall directly above the Pharaoh's head where six baboons, representing Toth, the god of wisdom, were pictured squatting on what appeared to be bright red apples.

"Ah, you see," she said smiling, "it goes on even after death."

THE PALACE OF QUEEN HATSHEPSUT

The Arabs call it *Deir el Bahari,* meaning "the monastery of the north," remembering that in the early years of Christianity a community of monks settled in these columned halls. We call it the funerary monument of Queen Hatshepsut, which is not much more illuminating. Certainly she was buried somewhere near here, but what she built was something so ravishingly different from anything that can be seen in the Valley of the Kings that it is as though she still lives there, still haunts the colonnades, and is still carried in her gold palanquin up and down the steps to a palace nestling under the hills.

Deir el Bahari is only three-quarters of an hour's walk from the Valley of the Kings but the landscape has abruptly changed. There is no longer a maze of deep valleys. Instead there are steep and rugged cliffs four hundred feet high and a broad plain stretching down to the Nile. At the very foot of the cliffs the Queen built three gleaming white terraces, like arms opening to the sky. Once there was an avenue of sphinxes leading to these terraces. They have vanished but no harm has been done. The plain is green with young barley, donkeys amble along the lanes between the fields, smoke comes from the village huts, an occasional automobile speeds along the highway, and there, straight in front of you, appearing to hover above the surface of the earth, stands one of the loveliest palaces ever built for the living or the dead. The Queen chose the site marvelously well, and her architect Senenmut built it to perfection, having discovered exactly the right proportions for the three terraces. We know a good deal about Senenmut, who was plump and moon-faced, and who carried himself with the enormous dignity of a man who wields great power in the kingdom. He was far more than the court architect. He was so very close to the Queen that he was permitted to depict himself on the reliefs showing the principal events of her reign. Because he was the tutor of her daughter he was sometimes depicted holding the young princess on his lap.

Queen Hatshepsut was over forty when she came to the throne, but as she shows herself in her statues she is always youthful with delicate features, a broad forehead, a long slender nose, small lips, a small and firm chin, and a slender neck. The faintest of smiles seems to hover on her lips. The Pharaohs liked to show themselves in august majesty, conscious of their power and their magnificence. The Queen is more conscious of her beauty, her youthfulness, her charm. She was about fifty-five when she was portrayed kneeling at the feet of the supreme god Amun-Ra, looking like a particularly handsome boy of sixteen, smooth-chested, not muscular, her slender arms alone testifying to her femininity, for it was the custom to show the Pharaoh as a male, and accordingly she was sometimes portrayed wearing the artificial black plaited beard worn by the Pharaohs on public occasions. Though the sculptors probably flattered her, as the painters flattered Queen Elizabeth of England, there is no doubt that the Queen, fixed in her eternal youth, possessed a compelling beauty. Her astonishing palace nestling at the foot of the Theban hills was an abstract portrait of her, or so it seemed. Above all, she was vividly alive, tempestuous, inquisitive, cunning, imaginative, for she succeeded in maintaining her power for twenty-one years at a time when powerful forces were arraigned against her.

It was one of those days when the heat wells out of the sky, when the earth shudders and heaves under the sun's rhythmic hammer blows, and these reddish cliffs seemed to be churning out savage blasts of heat designed to kill us. Here was open ground; we had been happier in the coolness of Tutankhamen's tomb. Yet even when we were cursing the heat and the blinding glare of the processional ramp that led to the Queen's colonnades, we were aware of a dazzling beauty, of a setting too perfect to be true, of a soaring boldness of design. Drugged by the heat, blinded by sweat, scarcely knowing how we acquired the energy to walk up the ramp, we paused from time to time to observe the palace above us until at last we collapsed in the shelter of the columns.

On reflection we decided that it was all very simple, and we should have thought of it the moment we set eyes on it. It was only now, while huddled in the shade, recovering from the long march up the ramp, that the full glory of the place occurred to us. It was as though the sunlight had fixed on our sensitized brains the image of the temple and the processional way as seen from a distance, fixing it so indelibly that even when we were inside the temple we continued to see it as though we were still walking toward it. Solange was leaning on one of the pillars with one arm raised to protect her eyes from the dazzling light beating up from the white limestone.

"*Comme un oiseau,*" she said. "Like a bird with wings stretched out—"

"Resting from the heat?"

"Oh no, the heat has nothing to do with it. The bird is always there. The wings are outspread. It is ready for flight."

She went on talking in her sing-song voice about this temple-palace, smiling to herself, standing there exactly as though she was part of the decoration of the colonnade. What she was saying was something that all of us had already observed: the temple was the image in stone of a white bird which had settled at the foot of the red rocks. It was also, of course, many other things, just as Solange herself was many people. As she stood there framed between the columns, I thought it was time she put on a small black beard, for she looked remarkably like Queen Hatshepsut. And when, having recovered a little from the heat, she walked along the colonnade swinging her skirt, she had the air of having just stepped down from one of the carvings on the walls of the palace.

These carvings were in light relief, and here and there the original red paint still clung to them. There were the ceremonial carvings in which the Queen is seen adoring Amun-Ra, but there are also the carvings in which she celebrated two exploits that evidently gave her great pleasure. One of these was the raising of two enormous granite columns at Karnak in her honor, and the other was an expedition she sent to Punt in search of myrrh trees to be planted in the gardens of her palace and whatever other valuable objects might be found there. She placed her treasurer Nehsi together with her favorite Senenmut in charge of five ships, filled the holds with valuable presents for the Prince of Punt, including a large statue of herself, and ordered them not to return until they had drawn up a treaty with the Prince and loaded the ships with treasure. The ships sailed along a canal joining the Nile to the Red Sea and apparently reached Punt, which was perhaps the coast of Somaliland, without incident. They were welcomed by the swarthy Prince and by his absurdly fat and ungainly wife, who is shown followed by a donkey, and there is an inscription reading: "This is a donkey—absolutely true," which was intended to convey the message that the donkey had carried the fat woman on its back and survived.

Poor Princess of Punt! And also, and more importantly, lucky Princess of Punt, to be immortalized as a living creature, preposterously fat, preposterously ugly, but possessing an enduring spark of life although she died about 3,500 years ago. Long before Akhnaten, the heretic Pharaoh, let loose the floods of the Egyptian imagination, the artists were already experimenting with a kind of happy caricature. They were magnificent portraitists with a sense of individual character. Unfortunately they were rarely permitted to exert their gift of caricature on the gods and Pharaohs. They could caricature the fat Princess of Punt with impunity, for she was a foreigner, a captive, and ridiculous.

Queen Hatshepsut reigned for twenty-one peaceful years that brought prosperity to Egypt, a fact that caused Solange to suggest that it would have been much better if all the Pharaohs had been women. Then she remembered Cleopatra. Her face fell. "What," she asked, "made Hatshepsut so wonderfully gifted in building palaces? Where are the other ones? Where is she buried? Is she here?" It appeared that she was not there: her successors detested her memory, scratched out her name wherever it appeared, built a casing round her obelisks at Karnak in order to hide them—the casings finally fell away, revealing them in all their perfection—and they went on to destroy her body. Queen Hatshepsut's nephew, Tuthmosis III, came to the throne, vowing vengeance against her. He destroyed everything except the important thing. The lovely funerary palace, like white sea-foam lapping at the foot of the cliffs, remains to testify to her taste, her power, and her beauty. The palace itself was an abstract portrait of the Queen, and very beautiful.

Not far away are the tombs of the nobles with brightly painted walls. We see the nobles riding and feasting, but there is something oddly amateurish and provincial in these paintings. Alas, the small boys who

Temple at Luxor

Temple at Karnak

Pyramid at Saqqara

Temple at Deir el Bahari

Mosque of Ibn Tulun, Cairo

Mosque of Ibn Tulun, Cairo

King Tutankhamen, Cairo Museum

Akhnaten, Cairo Museum

followed us into the tombs were trying to sell us amulets, scarabs and sphinxes, "which my uncle dug up yesterday in the sands." And these objects had a curious provincial and mass-produced look about them.

Noon came, the heat came relentlessly out of the sky, and you wondered why the body did not melt, why the Nile did not vanish into steam. The ferry was waiting for us, to take us back to the hotel in Luxor where we would eat and enjoy a siesta until it was cool enough to see the temples at Karnak. "Does the word luxury derive from Luxor?" Solange asked. Then she went off to sit on the prow of the little ferry-boat, looking like Cleopatra on her barge, twirling her blue and white parasol, with the Western Hills and the dead Pharaohs behind her.

THE SHADOWY TEMPLES

To reach the temples at Karnak you drive along the banks of the Nile by horse-carriage for about twenty minutes, protected against the evil eye by the many signs painted on the carriage and by the amulets worn by the horses. The drivers were boys who whipped the horses unmercifully. The road had many pot-holes and the springs of the carriages had perished long ago. Nevertheless it was a pleasant drive, for the Nile remained in view. It was the purest blue flecked with gold, cool and inviting, and the feluccas were gliding downstream with the grace and solemnity of swans.

We knew we were in trouble when we reached the great avenue of sphinxes and left the carriages to listen to the guide giving a brief lecture on the history of Karnak. He threw in a few dates and dynasties but most of the lecture consisted of a bitter attack on American and European archaeologists who had carried away all the most precious objects in the temples, leaving to the Egyptians only what was too heavy to carry away. He said that when we saw mutilated figures, we should remember that they had been mutilated by foreigners, never by Arabs or Egyptians. He was about twenty-four, tall, jowly, with a pencil-line mustache that he was continually caressing with his index finger, and he studied us with a look of detached arrogance. We were the sheep, and he was the shepherd. He looked at us in a way that suggested he would be pleased to lead us to the slaughterhouse.

What was puzzling was why he despised us so much, for we were not unruly, asked him few questions and never corrected him. We were the most commonplace crowd of tourists imaginable. A German pastor, a young married couple from France, an elderly Pennsylvania business man who had retired and was going alone round the world, an English nurse attached to a hospital in Cairo, a Lebanese professor, and three or four quiet and timid people who were a little frightened and clung together. I suspect he was brooding because none of us except the Pennsylvania business man, who wore a gold watch-chain, showed any signs of wealth and therefore there would be few tips. From the beginning we were in a state of rebellion.

He told us that not only had the archaeologists taken the greatest treasures out of Egypt but people were continually pilfering them and selling them at a great price. If all these stolen monuments were returned, then Egypt would be millions of dollars richer. We must realize that it is a privilege to be conducted through the temples, we must follow him closely, and obey his commands. It was absolutely essential that none of us stray from the path. So we followed him at a distance without enthusiasm, trying to pretend that he did not exist, and he kept a watchful eye on us and continually counted us. What he wanted—our instant obedience and our attention—was something we could not give him except haltingly, and what we wanted was to be rid of him. The advantages were all on our side because Karnak consists of many temples and thousands of columns, some of them three yards in diameter, and we could hide behind them.

What was strange was how the hate flared up, died down, and flared up again. He would shout: "You must now come here, please!" and some of us came, and some didn't. He was terrified that someone might be lost and went darting round the columns to spy out our hiding places. By this time some of the original group that had clustered round him had wandered away. He was becoming so nervous and ill-tempered that we were almost sorry for him.

Karnak in its present state resembles those engravings by Piranesi of Roman ruins so vast that men resemble ants crawling along their surface. The columns are larger, taller, more splendidly carved, and crowded more closely together than one might expect from seeing even the best photographs. Here and there, especially in the unreachable upper registers, the paint still adheres to the stone. The gods are being worshiped, the kings are riding to battle, the processions of prisoners are constantly being

formed, and slowly one comes to realize that these temples are really the
private chapels of the Pharaohs, who exult in their power, their majesty,
and their successful wars. How dark it is in this forest of columns, but also
how peaceful, how calm, how safe! Once these temples were roofed, and
only a frail unearthly light came through the clerestory windows. Almost
it was a submarine world, and even though all the columns carved in relief
were brilliantly painted, and lamps hung down from the roofbeams, nevertheless it must have given an impression of darkness and sudden explo-
sions of brilliant light. And quite clearly—for the architects were master
craftsmen—all this was done deliberately in such a way as to give extraordinary solemnity to the rituals enacted among the columns. The Egyptians adored processions. Columns of white-robed priests moved between
the columns, vanished, reformed, made offerings, saluted the gods, chanting incessantly, and the columns had the effect of magnifying echoes, so
that the voices were prolonged and the echoes floated away in the distance. The columns, by their sheer size, their monumentality, and their
grace, signified the overwhelming power of the gods and of the Pharaoh
who was the earthly representative of the supreme god Amun, once the
ram-headed divinity of the local cult and later the embodiment of the
mysterious power welling out of Thebes.

It is fashionable to decry the Egyptian temples for their overwhelming
size, but in fact they are quite small compared with western cathedrals.
At Karnak the Pharaohs sometimes built a new temple next to a temple
that already existed. This was hallowed ground, they saw no incongruity
in building one temple next to another, and they reveled in the opportunity to portray themselves on the columns and pylons. The effect is
somewhat as though the great cathedrals of Chartres, Beauvais, Laon and
Coutances were set down together cheek by jowl, each cathedral leading
to the next. Imagine them all in ruins, without roofs, with many of the
statues defaced but with most of the columns still springing from the
ground, and you have something comparable with the great complex of
temples at Karnak. Once you have sorted out the separate temples, there
comes a sense of order and astonishing fulfillment. The gods are well
served. The architects have accomplished their purpose in providing suitable places for them to reveal themselves and for the kings and priests to
walk in majesty.

Once you have become accustomed to those crowded columns, and once you realize that they were intended for processions and singing and sacred dances, then Karnak becomes eminently intelligible and satisfying, and the feeling of awe and confusion begins to vanish. Karnak becomes a playground for the gods and a place to loiter in. The high seriousness remains, but the sculptors who carved the reliefs on the columns were not always serious. They amused themselves by depicting the recognizable faces of priests and priestesses, some plump, some thin, and all of them filled with life.

Sometimes, guidebook in hand, we can almost hear the authentic accents of the Pharaohs as they proclaim their purposes within the halls of Karnak. Queen Hatshepsut caused two huge obelisks, each nearly a hundred feet high and weighing three hundred and fifty tons, to be erected in one of the courtyards. Originally the entire surfaces of the obelisks were plated with gold, and although the gold has long since gone, the inscription carved into the granite is wonderfully clear and the bold hieroglyphics can still be read. These were the words she ordered to be written on each obelisk:

> When they shall see my monument in later years, let them say, "This was made by me," and be careful lest you say: "I know not, I know not." This obelisk fashioned of gold was made at my orders. By my life and by the love of Ra and by the favor of my father Amun, who filled my nostrils with life and health, I wear the White Crown [of Upper Egypt] and I am diademed with the Red Crown [of Lower Egypt]. These two gods have granted their two life-spans to me. I rule over this land like the son of Isis. I am as powerful as the sun of Nu when the sun reposes on the Boat of the Morning and rests on the Boat of the Evening, when he places his mother and the uraeus goddesses in the Sacred Barge, for as long as the sky created by him remains firm and fixed.
>
> I shall exist for ever like the North Star, I shall remain in the life of Atum. Therefore of a truth these two enormous obelisks shine in my majesty, gleaming with gold, for the sake of my father Amun by the love I bear him and to perpetuate his name, that they may stand erect in the temple precinct for ever and ever. Each has been fashioned out of a single block of granite, without any joint or break. My majesty began this work in the fifteenth year [of her reign], on the first day of the month Mechir, and completed it in the sixteenth year during the month Mesori, making all together only seven months from the time it was hewn from the mountain.

We can feel even today the exultation of the Queen as she surveyed her two obelisks, which were in themselves beautiful works of art. So in August, 1470 B.C., when the Nile was overflowing its banks, the obelisks reached Thebes from the granite quarries of Assuan and were carried to the temple courtyard. She was so pleased with the successful accomplishment of this prodigious task that she decorated her funerary monument at Deir el Bahari with reliefs showing the raising of the obelisks at Karnak. One of the obelisks has fallen, and the upper part lies in the debris nearby. The other remains in all its immaculate beauty in the place where it has stood for nearly thirty-five centuries.

Of all that remains in Karnak this obelisk is the most completely satisfying object. The carving of the hieroglyphics had become in her time the purest decoration, and it is incomparably grander than the obelisks that have been transported to Rome, Paris, London and New York. Time has not touched it, and the hieroglyphics are as sharply incised as on the day they were carved. Her boast that her obelisks would stand for ever in the temple precincts had been half-fulfilled; for one remains, erect and powerful, quivering with its ancient life, in all its glory.

The guide with the heavy jowls was screaming at us again, but by this time no one was paying any attention to him. Finally, out of pity, we grouped ourselves around him to listen to a last flurry of vituperation. Once again we were told that we—the young married couple from France, the German pastor, the Pennsylvania business man, and the rest of us—we, of all people, were responsible for the ruins of Egypt, we had made them ruins, we were culpable, we were the destructive elements, the assassins of the temples. "You foreigners steal everything," he said. "All you have left us is our ruins!"

It was too much, and we burst out into a kind of nervous, flickering laughter, smiling at one another in the vast shadows of the ruins, a little unsure of ourselves but certain that we had discovered the key to the mystery. The man was mad. It was as simple as that. With a lordly wave of his hand, he said: "You will now go back to your horse-carriages. We shall return by way of the Ramesseum. That is the last item on the agenda."

And suddenly, without quite intending to do so, we staged a revolution. We did not go back to the carriages. Instead we wandered happily among the ruins, disregarding him, pretending he had no existence even when he shouted and screamed after us: "Come back, please! Come back, *please!* Go to the horse-carriages!" We were in no mood for horse-carriages. We wandered about Karnak at our leisure, as though it belonged to us, happy to be in those dark temples shot through and through with brilliant yellow beams of sunlight. It was a place to picnic in. It was a wonderful stage setting. The more accustomed you became to those huge columns, the less awesome they became. They were no longer intimidating; they were like friendly trees in a forest clearing. We galloped among them as though on horseback, while the guide's voice grew fainter and fainter in the distance.

There were no Russians on the airplane taking me back to Cairo. Just after take-off we saw below us something we never expected to see at Luxor—an enormous ring of sandbags in the desert sands, and in the middle of it a sleek, metallic blue anti-aircraft gun. For some mysterious reason the gun was aimed at the Western Hills, where the dead Pharaohs were sleeping.

CAIRO

After Luxor and the quietness of the desert and the Nile, Cairo comes like a sustained scream so loud and terrible that for a while you wonder how people can possibly live there. The traffic is murderous, the automobiles clatter so violently that it is evident that they are all falling apart, the traffic police are incompetent, half the buildings seem about to collapse, too many of the people look desperately poor, and there comes a moment when you are sure the city is about to disintegrate and fall into the Nile. And then a little while later you realize that the sustained scream and the relentless seething activity is a sign of vigor and that these people who are close to the earth know exactly what they are doing and are going about their work purposefully and intelligently, and all this chaos is merely the outward manifestation of an inner order.

In the old days under the Turks, the French and the British, Cairo possessed a highly stratified society. There were Sultans, Khedives, Governor-generals, pashas, beys, and many other degrees of aristocracy, and all this vanished when King Farouk sailed away on his royal yacht. Since then crisis has followed crisis—the Cairenes would be very surprised if they woke up one morning and discovered there was no crisis—but the most intolerable crisis of all has been resolved. For centuries the Egyptians were ruled by foreigners. Now the foreigners have gone; they are their own masters; and since so little effective order is imposed on them from above, they can go about their affairs as chaotically as they please. A special kind of inspired confusion is a sign of democratic progress.

So in that steaming, frothing, reverberating city, with its winding, dusty sidestreets, overcrowded and evil-smelling, and its occasional avenues smelling of diesel fuel, there is always the sense of prodigious human activity. Mostly, of course, it is the prodigious human activity needed to earn a bare living. The Cairenes work hard but their hearts are not so much in work as in mere survival. They soon discover that the largest and wealthiest city in Africa will do very little to help them: they must make their own opportunities. They are adept at making opportunities where none previously existed. They are continually inventing new and hitherto unsuspected ways of earning money; they thrive on the new, the unexpected, the impossible, the accidental. They rejoice in going from A to B by way of X, Y and Z. They have a special affection for the accidental. Charms, spells, dreams, and soothsayers are all placed in the service of the desirable accident. If this fails, the Cairene begins all over again. He has more faith in the efficacy of charms than in the efficiency and effectiveness of his political leaders. Charms, like the blue beads worn by children against the evil eye, are the weapons that hammer accidents into a desirable shape.

Consider how Cairo was brought to birth by Jawhar al-Siqilli, who led the Fatimid army against the small town of Fustat, conquered it, and set about building a new city. The general was not an Egyptian. He was by birth a Greek who had lived in Sicily before being captured and enslaved by the Arabs. Having conquered Fustat, it remained to him to mark out the boundaries of the new capital of Egypt, and this he did by erecting poles strung together with ropes over a wide area. Thousands of workmen were standing by, ready to start digging when the signal was given. The astrologers were working on the horoscope of the city to establish the most auspicious moment for its nativity. When they had finally decided on the exact moment, the little bells attached to the ropes would begin to ring.

Unfortunately a raven flew down, sat on a rope, and set all the bells ringing long before the astrologers had made their decision. The astrologers were all the more terrified because at the moment when the bells started ringing, Al Kahira (Mars) was in the ascendant. This was a bad omen. At all costs the work must be stopped. It was too late. Reluctantly the astrologers agreed to let the work continue and thereafter the city was known as Al Kahira, or Cairo. Once again the accidental had been hammered into a desirable shape.

The raven alighted on the evening of May 5, A.D. 969, according to the chronicles. In theory Cairo was the capital of the vast Fatimid empire stretching from Cordova to Mosul. In fact the separate parts of the empire were breaking away; and to his sovereign, the Caliph of Cordova once wrote the most insolent of letters. It was very short. It said: "Thou ridiculest us because thou hast heard of us. If we had ever heard of thee, we would reply."

The sovereign of the Arab world, the Caliph Al Aziz, was one of the wisest and most beneficent of men, but the real ruler of the empire was the Sicilian Jawhar al-Siqilli, who built the great mosque called Al Azhar, meaning "the shining one," in honor of Fatima, the daughter of Muhammad. The mosque included a university, which to this day remains the hub of the intellectual life of Cairo and the source of a vast outpouring of Islamic studies. Jawhar died in A.D. 992, and four years later the Caliph died. His heir was the thirteen-year-old Caliph Al Hakim, who was more than half mad. He inherited the blue eyes and fair skin of his Russian mother. From the beginning of his reign he showed a ferocious intolerance. He murdered at leisure, ordered the destruction of churches and synagogues, leveled the Church of the Holy Sepulchre, forbade pilgrimages, uprooted the vineyards, prohibited banquets, music and chess, and even promenades along the Nile, and set old women to spy on young women and report what they discovered to the secret police. In his lucid moments he was intelligent and charming, but there were not many lucid moments. He fell in love with the grey ass which took him on his solitary wanderings, and announced that henceforth anyone maltreating an ass should be beaten almost to death. He fell in love with himself and concluded that he was divine and sent out missionaries to proclaim his divinity. One evening in February, A.D. 1021, he rode out to his observatory on the Muqattam hills and was never seen again. The ass was found with its forelegs hacked off, and blood marks led to a hollow where they found the Caliph's clothes, bloodstained, pierced by daggers, but carefully buttoned up. There was no sign of a body.

Al Hakim resembled those murderous emperors of mixed blood who haunt the pages of history and especially of Egyptian history, and who appear to have been sent down to earth like plagues, to remind men of their mortality. No sooner had one bloodthirsty conqueror sailed up the Nile, established a reign of terror, and been overthrown than another appeared. The Cairenes I knew were well aware they were the heirs of a tumultuous and bloody history. Strangely they rarely talked about the Pharaohs. In their eyes pharaonic Egypt was too far away and too inconsequential to throw any light on the present. But they loved to talk about the Fatimids and the Mamelukes and would discuss with easy tolerance the ferocious aberrations of Caliphs and Sultans.

Napoleon came, settled in a palace on the site of Shepheard's hotel, imagined he was Pharaoh, gave orders in his most imperious manner, and vanished like the morning mist. So did most of the conquerors. The Egyptians shrugged their shoulders, smiled wryly, and went on with their own affairs. Salvation lay in the family, in friends, in Islam. In guarded moments they mocked their conquerors. Polite, civilized, humorous, close to desperation, they were masters of camouflage and indirection. They have possessed a civilization much longer than any other people on earth and they have long ago concluded that the truth is elsewhere, nothing can be known for certainty, and history is something to be endured.

Today as you wander through Cairo in the dark, gluey, acid haze caused by the boiling fumes of Russian gasoline, you are aware of a society in a state of effervescence. The grandeur remains in the faces of the people, in the wonderfully carved minarets of the Mameluke mosques, in the pyramids, and in the treasures in the museums. The Pharaoh Ramses II stands outside the railroad station, and is not out of place. He is stern, implacable, larger than life or hope, and stands there as the representative of all those conquerors who made the lives of the people miserable. It seems only yesterday that the Albanian adventurer Mehemet Ali stormed into Cairo, offered a truce to his enemies, and then massacred them, founding a dynasty which ended only with the pathetic Farouk, enormously fat, sunk in torpor, his delicate jeweled hands fluttering over the instruments of power. He, too, was murderous and unscrupulous, and was easily forgotten.

In a crowded street you will see a face that reminds you instantly of Pharaoh, or another that reminds you of the dancers on the ancient tomb paintings. In their manners, their gestures, and their way of thought, they are much closer to pharaonic Egypt than they realize. They have a grace which is not easily forgotten, and now at long last they are in command of their destiny.

THE VIRGIN'S TREE

Behold, the angel of the Lord appeareth to Joseph in a dream, saying, Arise, and take the young child and his mother, and flee into Egypt, and be thou there until I bring thee word: for Herod will seek the young child to destroy him.

When he arose, he took the young child and his mother by night, and departed into Egypt. And was there until the death of Herod: that it might be fulfilled which was spoken of the Lord by the prophet, saying, Out of Egypt have I called my son.

The Gospel according to St. Matthew says nothing more about the journey to Egypt. The holy family took flight from Israel and returned only after the death of Herod. To the delight of the Renaissance painters Mary could be imagined riding on an ass and cradling the Christ-child in her arms, while Joseph walked beside her; and in their loneliness and helplessness there can be seen the tragedy of quite ordinary people fleeing from tyranny.

The apocryphal Gospel of the Infancy adds very little more information. We see the Christ-child performing a succession of improbable miracles. A man transformed into a mule becomes a man again when the child is placed on his back. An innkeeper recently married cannot enjoy his wife but is cured of his frigidity when the holy family comes to stay in the inn. We learn too that the holy family remained three years in Egypt, spent some time in Memphis, saw Pharaoh, "and in Matariya the Lord caused a well to spring forth, in which Mary washed his coat."

Matariya, now a suburb of Cairo, formerly part of the great city of

Heliopolis, has a small church said to be built on the site where the holy family took lodgings. There is an aged sycamore tree, a well, a courtyard, where it is very peaceful. The church has some execrable wall-paintings narrating the flight to Egypt, which must have been painted during the last twenty years. It is a small church, rather sombre, memorable chiefly because there were so many lilies on the altar that we gasped at the sweetness of the perfume. An old Copt with a nut-brown handsome face, thick white eyebrows and intelligent eyes accompanied us as we examined the terrible wall-paintings.

"Have you seen the sycamore tree?" he asked.

Yes, we had seen it.

"And the well?"

Yes, we had seen that, too.

He nodded and sucked in his lips.

"What do you think? Is it really the tree under which Mary and Joseph and the Christ-child rested?"

I said something about the permanence of legends and traditions. I imagined that in Egypt traditions were maintained for thousands of years, and it was not at all impossible. The tree was obviously very old and gave a good deal of shade. The old man sighed.

"So many stories," he said. "We don't even know when it all started. Perhaps at the time of the Crusaders, perhaps earlier. I have read somewhere that there *was* a sycamore tree, but it died in 1670 and a new one was planted on exactly the same spot. I suppose the truth is that we don't really know anything at all about the holy family's stay in Egypt—nothing at all!"

I suggested there was nothing improbable in their coming to Matariya, nor was there anything improbable in the story that they rested under the shade of a sycamore tree.

"So you think it is true?"

"No, but it is possible to believe it."

"How can you believe when there is no proof, when for example one tree died and another tree takes its place, and it is only a legend, and not even a legend. It says they came to Egypt, and that is true, for it is in the Gospel, but it does not say anywhere where they stayed or how they lived. Absolutely nothing! So we have all these legends, and only God knows where the truth is!"

So he spoke in the shade of the sycamore tree, a devout man, a Copt, wearing a striped gown and straw sandals, indistinguishable from any other Egyptian except for the intelligence that blazed from his eyes. I never learned what his business was. I think he was simply someone who lived close to the church and had by chance entered it just as we arrived.

He spoke about the Copts with justifiable pride as "people who have suffered much and survived." Who were they? How many were they? How did they differ from the other Egyptians? He shrugged his shoulders again. "We are the people nobody knows," he said sadly. "We have learned to remain silent." They were outside the three major streams of Christianity—the Orthodox, the Catholic and the Protestant—and observed a form of religion which must be very close to early Christianity. They had not intermarried with the Arab conquerors of Egypt, and therefore preserved the features of the ancient Egyptians. They were Monophysites, believing that Christ had one nature, and were therefore regarded by the Orthodox Church as heretics. When Egypt became a Byzantine dominion ruled from Constantinople, the Copts were savagely persecuted for their heresy and some of the worst atrocities were committed when the Byzantines were reeling from the attacks of the Arabs, their huge armies torn to pieces by a handful of Arab invaders.

The old Copt was saying like a litany: "We are the lost ones, we are the silent ones." He spoke without complaining. Once he said: "Christ came to Egypt like a gentle wind, like a spirit, but where he set down his feet no one knows."

Later in the day I found a copy of Edward William Lane's book *The Manners and Customs of the Modern Egyptians,* first published in 1836 and still the best introduction to the Egyptian character. Lane has a chapter on the Copts, but has little to say about their history. It was an eventful history, and some of the most eventful hours occurred when in A.D. 640 the Arabs stormed across the desert and attacked Babylon, a city built on the ruins of Heliopolis. In command of Babylon was Cyrus, Viceroy of Egypt and Patriarch of Alexandria, who hated the Copts, feared the Arabs and adored his double role of spiritual and earthly ruler of Egypt.

Cyrus provides an interesting study of the corrupt ruler confronted with sudden terrifying dangers, those dangers which at first he hardly suspects and realizes at an increasing momentum. The small Arab army outside the walls of Babylon was ill-equipped to conquer a city. It had only the most primitive weapons: no siege engines, no battering rams, no towers, no Greek fire. Cyrus had twenty-thousand well-equipped troops, and the Arabs had a raggle-taggle army of thirty-five hundred men. They also had a commanding general, Amr ibn-al-As, who believed that his army was unconquerable. The Arabs offered three alternatives to Cyrus: he could fight to the death, he could become a vassal paying tribute to the Arabs, or he could embrace Islam. He vacillated, tried to buy them off, attempted to prolong the negotiations in the hope that the Arabs would go away and leave him alone. Amr sent a Negro called Ubadah ibn-al-Samit to discuss terms with Cyrus, who fell into a rage and exclaimed: "Take that black man away! I won't discuss terms with him!" This was a mistake, and the Arabs who accompanied Ubadah were quick to point out that the Negro belonged to the select group known as the Companions of the Prophet who were held in especially great honor among the Arabs. Cyrus turned to one of his followers and said: "I very much fear that God has sent these men to devastate the world!"

There appeared to be a mysterious traitor in Babylon. He was called "the Makaukus" and was thought to be a Copt who had his own reasons for detesting the Byzantines. The Makaukus was trying desperately to surrender the city to the Arabs. Who was he? Even the Arabs did not know. In the last years of the nineteenth century an English scholar, A. J. Butler, who came to Egypt to tutor the Khedive's children, solved the problem. It was like a detective story, for clues abounded and were only waiting to be discovered. The Makaukus was Cyrus.

Finally Cyrus reluctantly accepted the least painful of the three alternatives: tribute. Amr let him go to Alexandria and so to Constantinople to seek the Byzantine emperor's agreement. Not unexpectedly the Emperor refused and ordered Cyrus to be banished and Alexandria placed in a state of readiness. For a little while longer Babylon remained under the command of the Byzantines.

In that long humid summer, only eight years after the death of the Prophet Muhammad, the army of Islam camped outside the walls of Babylon, waiting for the city to fall. Amr was in no hurry. In the intervals of planning further campaigns he wrote voluminous letters to the Caliph, the Prophet's successor, who was unable to comprehend how a whole nation could depend for its life on a single river. "Tell me about Egypt," the Caliph wrote, and Amr answered:

O Commander of the Faithful, Egypt is no more than a desert with two ranges of hills, the one in the West resembling sand dunes, the other like the belly of a lean horse. Between these hills flows the Nile: blessed are its morning and evening journeys. For the Nile has its seasons of rising and falling, following the courses of the sun and the moon, and causes milk to flow, and gives abundant life to cattle. When the springs and fountains are let loose, then the swelling waters flood the fields on either side, and all the villages are cut off from one another so that the villagers must travel in coracles or frail boats or shallops light as the evening mist. And when the river has risen to the full, it sinks back again, and that is the time when the people who have learned to plow the earth so well gather the fruit of their labor; and their labor is very light. So the crop is grown, and the water is the source of the nourishment.

Therefore, O Commander of the Faithful, you can understand how Egypt is sometimes the color of a white pearl, and then like golden amber, and then like a green emerald, and then like a carpet of many colors.

Amr's letter tells us a good deal about the richness of the Arab imagination. He wrote a hymn to the Nile, omitting, in the eyes of the Egyptians, one important aspect. The Egyptians never saw the river alone, but always in the arms of the Sun. For Amr, the thickset, black-bearded conqueror from the desert, the Sun was only a small lamp in the heavens, and Allah was greater than all the Suns.

Soon Babylon fell, and in his leisurely fashion Amr led his ragged army to Alexandria. Alexandria was then the most powerful naval base in the world, a thriving seaport, with sumptuous gardens and colonnaded streets. Here Alexander the Great lay in a crystal sarcophagus; here Cleopatra died and St. Mark was martyred. The city fell with almost no struggle, but to the very end the Byzantines were persecuting the heretical Copts. When Amr entered in triumph, he found near the gates a crowd of Copts whose hands had been cut off and who welcomed the Arabs with their bleeding stumps.

I think of the bleeding stumps and the Virgin's tree and the overwhelming perfume of the lilies massed on the altar of an ugly church, but more often I think of the old Copt with handsome features and the eyes glowing with intelligence, who said: "Christ came to Egypt like a gentle wind, like a spirit, but where he set down his feet no one knows."

THE CITY OF THE SUN

The Greeks called this city Heliopolis, and in the Bible it is called On, which is much closer to its original name. Scholars believe it was called Ein-re under the Pharaohs. Of this once great city, dedicated to the worship of the Sun, nothing remains except a single obelisk rising in a beanfield in the suburbs of Cairo not far from Matariya.

The sun-god Re shared with the sun-god Amun of Thebes an unchallenged supremacy; they became the same god Amun-Ra; they were the rulers of Egypt, and the Pharaohs regarded themselves as the earthly representatives of the supreme god. At Heliopolis the Phoenix was born and died and was born again from its flaming nest. Herodotus visited the city and talked with the shaven-headed priests, Plato studied at its university, and Strabo, the philosopher and geographer, passed through it in 25 B.C. and wrote: "I saw the large houses where the priests lived, for they say that in ancient times the priests congregated here to study philosophy and astronomy, but the congregations have now dispersed and their studies have ended. The houses of the priests were pointed out to us and we saw the studios of Plato and Eudoxus, who both passed thirteen years here with the priests, according to some writings I have seen."

Where there was a thriving city and armies of priests, there was now a beanfield tended by a farmer, who was very old, and by two archaeologists, who were very young. They had dug a small trench near the obelisk and in the drenching heat they were wondering whether to enlarge it, dig deeper, or start somewhere else. The obelisk loomed above them, greyish white, superbly venerable. Time had smoothed much of the inscription but most of it can still be seen, especially if you stand at an angle to it. I asked the young archaeologists whether they could read it, but they shook their heads. "We are archaeologists," one of them said. "We are not trained to read hieroglyphics."

"What are you trained for?"

"To discover the past."

"Well, shouldn't you learn to read what the past is saying?"

For some reason the younger of the two burst out into a frenzy of laughing. He was almost doubled up with laughter. There were people who knew about archaeology and people who knew about hieroglyphics; the important thing was to be *practical* if you were an archaeologist. As for the learned men who read inscriptions, they rarely agree about the meaning of the words they have so laboriously transcribed and interpreted. He showed me his notebook which showed the plan of the trench and its precise measurements. "In any case," he added, "this is just a trial dig. On was not very important and we don't expect to find anything. It is quite a small place." He pointed to a low rise a few hundred feet away, a raised road and an embankment, and from these landmarks he thought it was possible to distinguish the size of a very small town. "Quite small —almost insignificant," he shrugged, and went on digging.

It was a very hot day, the earth steamy, and the only sound came from the two young archaeologists widening their trench. Usually they get laborers to do their digging for them, and it was surprising that they should be laboring so hard. I was expecting treasure to come pouring out of the earth, but none came. What puzzled me most of all was that they knew so little about On, its wealth and power. It could not possibly have been contained within the low rise, the road and the embankment. We know it had high walls, palaces, many temples, law-courts, colleges and dormitories for the students who flocked to the city from all over Egypt. It emerged into prominence at the end of the Fourth Dynasty, about 2750 B.C., as the cult city of Re, the Sun in Glory, represented by a falcon. The Pharaohs of the Fifth Dynasty included the name of the god in their titles, enlarged the temples, showered wealth on them, moved in procession to the inner sanctum, the holy of holies, where Re was exhibited in golden splendor, but only to the eyes of the Pharaoh and the high priest, who bore the title of Great Seer. Here were elaborated the sacred texts of Re, which were included in *The Book of the Dead*. Here, too, was the sacred lake from which the sun emerged trembling on the water, new born each day, and this lake is commemorated in the name of the local village Ain Shams, which means "the fountain of the sun." But the lake vanished long ago, the white-robed priests have long since departed, and there remains only this solitary column to remind the visitor that he is standing in a place that was holy for nearly three thousand years.

I could not read the hieroglyphics and it was many years later before I learned that it had been erected by Sesostris I to commemorate the jubilee of his reign. The inscription, repeated on all four sides of the obelisk, is less interesting than others erected by him in which he proclaims his own majesty and beauty and pronounces that they will be remembered in all the ages to come. "My fame is in the obelisk, my fame is in the lake," he wrote, meaning that he would be remembered by his monuments and because he worshiped at the sacred lake. Once the obelisks were capped with gold plate and blazed like fire in the sun. Even now, pitted by forty centuries of wind and sand, the obelisk, which was sixty feet high, maintained its absolute dignity. Almost it was an abstraction of the power and beauty of the ancient city.

I wandered around the beanfield, annoyed with myself because it was quite impossible to imagine the city and just as impossible to imagine how it could vanish so completely. At last I went back to the young archaeologists to ask them whether they had discovered anything. They were deep in the trench, they had discovered nothing, and they were out of temper.

"It's all a waste of time," the younger one said. "We are digging in the wrong place. The damned trench is filling up with water."

He clambered out of the trench, grotesquely angry as he looked at his mud-stained trousers and thought of all the wasted hours he had spent there.

"Did you find anything?" I asked. "Anything at all?"

"The damned water table is so high we'll never find anything. Think of the cost of draining it! No, I'll report that the preliminary excavations are a complete failure!"

I looked into the trench. There, deep down, flashing with a hundred suns, bubbling out of the earth, was the lake of the sun.

THE SUMMITS OF TIME

The dragoman was at least seventy years old, fat and jowly, with little black eyes embedded in folds of flesh and an old man's mouth that looked as though it was dreaming of succulent and crystallized fruit. He had a sweet tooth, ate prodigiously, and consumed enormous quantities of sweet tea. In his flowing bournous, his great paunch making it belly out like a sail in a high wind, he looked like a sheikh of Araby who perpetually indulged in feasts and concubines, but his looks belied him. In fact he was a rather timid person, rather quiet, not very happy, hating old age and lost in the new, vibrant Cairo around him. He could remember a time when there were few automobiles in the streets and the horse-carriages with silk curtains flew past in clouds of dust and the British flag waved over the Citadel. There was a time when he had been a kind of major-domo to Colonel Sanderson, who was evidently an important figure in the political agency ruling Egypt.

"There were dances every night," he said. "Fashionable women with soft skins—at least a hundred of them. House boats on the Nile, too. No hurrying about. Very calm the English were. Polite, too. They were all gentlemen. Colonel Sanderson once told me I was the only gentleman he had met among the Egyptians. Of course he was trying to flatter me, but I suppose in my own way I was trying to be a gentleman." He went on a little later: "Poor Colonel Sanderson! He drank like a fish, but never before sundown! That was a rule with him—drunk every night and sober in the morning! He had great power and could get anything done! I suppose if he wanted the Pyramids removed to Thebes, or something like that, he could have got it done! And full of kindness! When he retired from the Army he went to live in Bournemouth, and he wrote to me and sent me presents every Christmas. Once he sent me a postcard saying he was not feeling well and they had put him in a bathchair, and then there were no more postcards. I suppose he died, poor fellow."

As I wandered around Cairo, Colonel Sanderson, long dead, and Achmed Naguib, very much alive, were my constant companions. I went in and out of mosques and museums and antique shops, and they were always at my side. They were comforting presences, and sometimes they seemed as old as the Pharaohs.

One day we drove to Saqqara to see the stepped pyramid of King Zoser, the first pyramid known to history and also the first stone building of great size known to have been built on the earth. We swung out past Mena House and the pyramids of Gizeh while Achmed Naguib chattered about Colonel Sanderson and all the other distinguished British officers he had known. They were nearly all dead, and he would usually end his recital with the soft comment: "I suppose he died, poor fellow." But when we came close to the stepped pyramid deep in the desert, a faint wind stirring the powdery sand and the heat blazing out of the cloudless sky, the landscape throbbing with the pulsations of heat as though everything visible had somehow been transformed into a drumhead which was being hammered incessantly, he became once more the perfect Egyptian drago-man, interpreter and guide, but now he was vigorously fanning himself with a Japanese fan.

He knew a good deal about the excavations in Saqqara and especially about that beautiful pyramid with its six stages, rust-red and rosy in the afternoon light. I suppose I must have read about it and seen pictures of it, but as we walked ankle-deep in the sand, I was taken completely by surprise. Time had removed the smooth coating of white limestone, it has rounded the edges, and most of the palaces, chambers and temples that once clustered at its feet have fallen into ruins. But this stepped pyramid, two hundred feet high and about four hundred feet wide, was one of the most beautiful structures in creation, possessing a power and majesty which even now after nearly five thousand years can make the heart sing. Long before the city of On was built a superb architect had calculated the proportions of the six stages of the pyramid to give an effect of growth, of springing life. It is not a dead thing, like the pyramid of Cheops. It has the beauty of living form and inexhaustible life, a certain gentleness and modesty. The three pyramids at Gizeh abruptly pierce the sky, asserting themselves against the heavens. The stepped pyramid at Saqqara climbs into the sky by stages and each stage is a rung in the ladder.

Achmed Naguib knew all the facts and figures, the exact height, the exact length of the base, the name of the architect, which was Imhotep, and the date when it was built, which was about 2650 B.C. The whole pyramid was built of bricks, which had the colors of fire in them, and therefore there was none of the appalling labor of hoisting huge mono-lithic stones up inclined planes. Originally there had been quite a small pyramid, but it had grown, as Aztec and Mayan pyramids sometimes grew, by being buried under a larger pyramid and then under another. The pyramid is the monument of King Zoser whose wonderful gaunt and ravaged statue stands in the Cairo Museum. Time has ruined the imperi-ous face so that it resembles a mask with hollowed out eyes, smashed nose, jutting cheekbones, prominent lips, and a long black beard. It is the earliest life-size portrait of a king that has come down to us, and even in its ravaged state it is one of the best.

Looking at this statue, we have the feeling that we know him well, for he haunts our dreams. He has much to say, and says it more sternly than his innumerable successors: about divine kingship, about autocracy, about the triumph of the will. He is not a man to be trifled with or even to be argued with. We see him again in some reliefs found at Saqqara showing him running nearly naked, crowned, holding the flail and the crook, symbols of his authority, as he takes part in one of those ceremonial races designed to show that he was in full command of his vital energy. He has powerful shoulders, a thin waist, and long thin legs without any fat on them. Naked, he looks as kingly as he appears in the painted limestone statue in the museum.

The pyramid at Saqqara is a work of quite extraordinary accomplish-ment. So, too, was the temple erected at the foot of the pyramid, where for the first time we see the lotos columns and the frieze of cobra heads that were symbols of kingship. All round the pyramid and enclosed by a thirty foot high wall were palaces and pavilions, courtyards and colonnades for the dead king to wander in. There were chapels and altars where the priests made their offerings. There were pools where the king could bathe and trees where he could take shelter from the sun, although his body was buried nearly a hundred feet below the level of the earth. For the ancient Egyptians a dead king was a contradiction in terms: he died, but remained deathless. He was robed with immortality like the Sun. This pyramid surrounded by its vast, high-walled courtyard was therefore an abstract portrait of King Zoser, a supreme evocation of kingly majesty.

Once, when the six-staged pyramid was covered with smooth polished white limestone, it must have been even more breathtaking than it is today. It flashed fiercely in the sunlight, shimmering and blazing with an unearthly glow, dazzling in its immensity, superb as the summits of time. Archaeologists have been able to restore some of the temple precincts within the courtyard; the lines and proportions are clear-cut, very modern, very crisp. And all this was fashioned at the very beginning of art, at the dawn of history.

We walked among the colonnades of a restored temple where the columns were springing up: the first columns, the first king, the first pyramid. Achmed Naguib was saying: "Colonel Sanderson never liked the pyramids. He said they were too big—just lumps of stone. It's a great pity, effendi, that more people do not come to see our pyramids."

THE TOMB OF LORD MERERUKA

The sand was as soft and fine as silk, drifting carelessly even though there was no wind, lapping the tombs of the nobles who served the court at Memphis, the great city which has now vanished among the date palms. Memphis was about five miles away, and all the area around it was once cultivated fields and there were straight roads leading to the tombs of the nobles. Now you must walk ankle-deep through the waving sheets of sand, and you can pretend you are in the middle of the desert. Happily, with the aid of four poles and corrugated iron roofing, someone has erected a lemonade stand in the shadow of King Zoser's pyramid. It is the modern oasis; there is even ice; the sound of fizzy lemonade being poured into a glass is like the sound of rain on the parched desert.

From this shelter King Zoser's pyramid can be seen without glare, beautiful and mysterious, rising above walls of sand, russet and red and glowing pink, not in the least austere. Like many great monuments it has improved with age and has become warm and companionable. Once it had sharp edges, clean contours; the winds of fifty centuries have rounded them and torn away the thin coating of white Tura limestone that once gleamed like marble. I tell myself that of all the things I have seen in Egypt this ruined pyramid and Queen Hatshepsut's palace nestling at the foot of the red Theban hills are the most impressive, and for the same reasons. They have the quality of intense living form, an urgent quivering life flows through them. Again and again there is this sense of the quickening of life, as though these ancient people had enjoyed life so much that they were able to project their enjoyment far into the future.

The Egyptians through the centuries have given a full measure of reverence to Imhotep, who designed the pyramid. He was the vizier of King Zoser as well as his chief architect. He was also a physician, a scribe, a moralist, and a high priest. He was a Renaissance man, a man so gifted that he can be compared with Leonardo da Vinci, and he was in fact the first man of superb intelligence known to history. When the Greeks came to trade with Egypt, they found that Imhotep was being worshiped as the god of medicine and they identified him with Aesclepius; at the same time he was the god of literature, and every scribe would pour a libation to him before sitting down to write. They made statues of him, prayed to him, placed offerings before him. What was enchanting about the statues was that they portrayed him as a young man, almost a boy, gazing into the distance deep in thought while he holds a sheet of papyrus on his knees.

I was still gazing at the pyramid when the guide said: "You can't simply sit there looking at the pyramid for the rest of the day. There's too much to see."

He had quenched his thirst. There were five bottles of lemonade on the wooden bench. He ordered a sixth. There was no one else in the shelter except the old man who served the drinks. It was very quiet and restful, and I saw no reason to leave this marvelous place from where you could see nothing except the drifting sand and the pyramid that was changing color at every moment.

"Come, effendi, it is time to go," he said. "There are marvelous tombs here."

I said I did not want to see any more tombs. The tombs in the Valley of the Kings were far less interesting than Queen Hatshepsut's palace with the wonderful arms opening out to the sun. It was better to be in the open air than down among the tombs.

"There are hundreds of tombs," he went on. "Very beautiful, very well painted."

I said I was not going to see a hundred tombs. He lifted a warning finger.

"You will be sorry, effendi, if you don't see them."

"What is effendi?"

"It is a term of respect. It is like calling you lord. If you miss the tombs, then afterwards you will say that I did not show you the best things. I have had the honor of guiding many distinguished people to Saqqara and they have always been grateful to me for showing them the tombs."

So we walked for ten minutes across the sand in the furnace heat until we came to the mastaba of Lord Mereruka. *Mastaba* means "bench" in Arabic, and these low squat tombs do have some faint resemblance to tables or benches. There is a door, which was once sealed, and steps lead down into the small pillared rooms where every wall is covered with reliefs carved in the limestone, many of them painted in brilliant colors, and sometimes the paint has flaked away, leaving only the gleaming marble-white surface.

Like Imhotep, Lord Mereruka had been a vizier. Also, like Imhotep, he was very much more, for he describes himself as the scribe of the divine books, inspector-general of the priests of the pyramid of King Teti, comptroller of the King's recording scribes, by which he meant that he was the chief historian, and overseer of the King's works, by which he meant that he was in charge of all the public works of the kingdom. He had married one of the King's daughters, and there is no reason to believe that he was not all that he claimed to be. The mastaba was erected during his lifetime and he supervised every detail of it.

Five hundred years had passed since the death of King Zoser. The grandeur of the Third Dynasty had gone; we were now in the Sixth Dynasty; religious fervor has given way to a cultivated humanism delighting in all the activities of man. There are at least a thousand representations of men at work and play on the walls of the mastaba. We see men wrestling, running, working in the fields, offering tribute to the King, preparing and attending feasts, or hunting the hippopotamus among the reeds. There is an astonishing sense of movement. A boy holds in front of him three or four geese grasped by their necks, and their feathers are fluttering violently. The cattle are not moving slowly; they hurry home, prodded by the herdsmen. Lord Merekura wanted to be remembered as a man who could be harsh on occasion, and so there were reliefs showing peasants being rounded up and beaten for non-payment of taxes, and he was apparently a man who encouraged physical sports, for there are many naked runners and wrestlers and jumpers. There are passages on these reliefs which are almost Greek in the natural portrayal of the male body; the muscles tense, the head held back, the arms rippling and the sweat gleaming. There are few female figures. The world he wanted to live in after his death was a predominantly male world.

We come to know Mereruka well, for he appears many times on the walls, usually holding his staff of office. He has rather heavy features, an underslung jaw, a prominent nose, enormous eyes and a broad forehead. He has a commanding presence, as befitted the chief minister in the kingdom. He is broad-shouldered, but when we see him clasping the hands of his two youthful sons, we observe that they are more broad-shouldered and have softer features. There is even—and this is the most startling thing in the tomb—a life-size statue of him emerging from a false door, naked except for the starched kilt which juts out in front; and he looks out on the world with grave distinction and imperious good humor.

Few of the individual figures are more than nine or ten inches high, and some of them are only one or two inches high, but all are brimming with life and movement. Calves leap playfully over one another, the heads of geese peer with a lively light in their eyes out of wickerwork baskets, the butcher flourishes his knife over the quivering flesh of the roped-up bull, and even the hippopotamus lurking among the reeds wear a surprised rueful air when confronted by the hunters. The gods are vastly outnumbered by the living. You have the feeling that you have come into the many-chambered house of a rich and powerful man who enjoyed his riches and the exercise of his power.

It was a supremely satisfying age. The gods were friendly, the earth was fertile, and men went about their affairs with pride in themselves and in their bodies. Seeing these people so lively in the tomb is to see life lived to the full. They are among the earliest relief carvings showing daily life in Egypt but already the technique has been completely mastered, the shapes of men and animals are delineated with remarkable accuracy, and each panel describes a single event, a single story. There are even captions provided in hieroglyphics, with scraps of conversation remembered from the past. A farm worker calls out to another: "What are you up to, lazybones?" The other replies: "The barley is very good today, young fellow." The caption provides a moral lesson and a warning against laziness. No laziness in the tomb?

The sand drifts into the tomb, the twilight descends on the shadowless world of the dead, while silence, like memory, wanders along the carved walls where only the red paint glows. Footsteps fall lightly in those square-walled chambers where a whole world is displayed in vivid figures cut out of gleaming limestone. Surprisingly, there is no solemnity. Quick, vivid action, the athletes running and wrestling, the cattle lowing and the geese honking. And there is Lord Merekura himself standing at the entrance, feet planted firmly on the ground, glowing with health, his diminutive full-breasted wives beside him, watching the young athletes at play.

We returned to Cairo toward evening through Memphis, the ancient capital, lost among the date palms, past a frowning Sphinx and a recumbent stone Pharaoh thirty feet long, past the desolate fields where the thin-boned cattle looked half as fat as the cattle on Lord Mereruka's walls and the villagers sat at the doors of mud-brick houses which have not changed for three thousand years or more. Coming out of the brightness of the desert into the darkness of the city was like passing from life into death. In all of Cairo was there anything as lively as Lord Mereruka and his two sons?

THE MOSQUE OF AHMAD IBN TULUN

If by some miracle I was set down in Cairo and told that I could spend only an hour there, I think I would immediately race to the Mosque of Ahmad Ibn Tulun. I have no affection for that murderous ruler who was the first since the time of the Pharaohs to rule over both Egypt and Syria, but I love his architect who designed with the simplest possible means a mosque that gives the impression of being erected for no other purpose except to celebrate the peace of God.

There is something very strange about the Mosque of Ahmad Ibn Tulun. What is strange is its absolute perfection, the absolute rightness of all its proportions. There is scarcely any ornamentation. There are no blue tiles, no richly decorated doors, no bulbous domes. There are four walls, a stone fountain, and a minaret twisted like a corkscrew. You would have thought that the corkscrew minaret would be out of place, but in this setting, just outside the mosque, it is perfectly appropriate, giving a sense of movement to the otherwise motionless courtyard. The stone fountain is pure decoration, for no Moslems ever made their ablutions there, and this was at the order of Ibn Tulun, who commanded that another ablution fountain should be built near the entrance to the mosque for the need of the worshipers. The fountain in the middle of the court-yard is of white stone, not pretentious, not particularly interesting. The beauty is in the great open courtyard surrounded on all sides by galleries pierced with pointed archways, the high walls crowned with a stone lacework that resembles the necks of swans or the arms of dancers. These pointed archways, among the earliest ever built, for the mosque dates from A.D. 876, give lightness to the immense courtyard. They are the ancestors of all Gothic arches. So as you wander along the shaded galleries, looking across the sun-baked courtyard, seeing the pointed arches on the other side, and exulting in the perfection of their proportions, you have the feeling that the world is calm and well ordered and a superb architect has succeeded in accomplishing the impossible—he has made out of four walls a feast for the eyes.

The story is told by al-Badawi that Ibn Tulun originally wanted to build a colonnade with three hundred columns, but where would he find the columns? He could take them from Christian churches, but this offered difficulties since the churches would probably fall down if their columns were removed, and for so vast a courtyard he needed so many columns. He had not the least intention of destroying all the churches of Egypt to decorate a single mosque. But what to do? A Christian architect wrote to Ibn Tulun, saying he could design a colonnade in such a way that it could be completed without a single column, and the only columns necessary in the mosque were two columns placed near the *mihrab* to help blind persons discover the direction of Mecca. The architect was brought into his presence. "Come, what is it you have to say about building the mosque?" he said, and the architect replied: "I will draw it for the Prince so that he can see it with his eyes—not a single column except the two near the mihrab!" Sheepskins were brought, pens, ink and rulers were supplied, and the architect drew his colonnade with the pointed arches, showing how these archways could be built of brick and then covered with plaster.

And so it was done. Ibn Tulun possessed an adventurous spirit, and did not care where good ideas came from as long as they were presented to him in good faith. His father was a Turkish slave captured by the Moslems in the wars of Central Asia. Handsome and intelligent, he came into the possession of the Governor of Bokhara who presented him to the Caliph Mamun. His son Ahmad became a favorite at court, received an excellent education, rose quickly in court circles, and in A.D. 869, when he was only thirty-four, he was appointed to the governorship of Egypt, whereupon he rebelled against the Caliph, pronounced Egypt an independent state, and ruled it with gusto. He built a new capital under the shadow of the Muqqattam Hills with a zoo, a race course, a polo ground, a palace for himself and another for his innumerable wives and concubines. He went on to build the first hospital in Cairo, which was paid for from the treasure found when one of his servants was riding in Upper Egypt and his horse stumbled into a pothole that opened to reveal more gold than anyone had seen since the time of the Pharaohs. Ibn Tulun was delighted. The gold paid for the erection of the hospital and there was enough left over to provide for its maintenance. The best doctors flocked to Cairo. Everything was free—medicines, nurses, food, the clothes worn by the patients. The hospital was kept scrupulously clean, and every Friday Ibn Tulun made a tour of inspection. According to the original grant, the hospital was maintained for everyone who needed it, but he took care that none of his soldiers and bodyguards were permitted to enter it for fear they would cause trouble. It was not that he distrusted his own soldiers, who were mostly slaves. It was simply that he had long ago come to the conclusion that soldiers are not very peaceful.

In a very short space of time Ibn Tulun rebuilt Cairo and transformed it into a brilliant, crowded capital. He died too soon to enjoy the full fruit of his inventiveness. He was only forty-nine when he caught acute dysentery from drinking too much buffalo milk. He rejected the advice of his doctors who begged him to go on a diet, and his last act as he lay dying was to order the doctors flogged to death because they had failed to cure him.

Of his twenty-nine children, sixteen sons and thirteen daughters, the least worthy of them succeeded to the throne. This was Prince Khumaraweh, whose love of luxurious self-indulgence exceeded that of the Caliph Harun al-Rashid. The trees in his garden were not beautiful enough; he coated them with gold. He built a house entirely lined in gold, filled it with wooden statues of himself and his wives dressed in cloth of gold, and sometimes slept on inflated leather pillows on an especially designed lake filled with quicksilver, lulled by the songs of his favorite singers or by the chanting of the *Koran* by the mullahs. One would have thought that sleeping on a lake of quicksilver, even when the leather pillows are moored by silken cords to silver columns, would be quite unsatisfactory, especially on nights of the full moon. The story would be almost unbelievable if it were not that traces of quicksilver have been found many years later.

Prince Khumaraweh wasted his substance. Handsome, elegant, depraved, and completely fearless, he wandered through life as though the whole of creation had been brought into existence for his enjoyment. He had a passion for lions, his favorite being a blue-eyed lion of great beauty and ferocity which habitually crouched at his feet, while he stroked it and brushed its coat and fed goats to it. All lions fed out of his hand. Sometimes it amused him to free the lions in his private zoo so that they could roam at liberty in the great courtyard; there would come a sudden roar, like the sound of an earthquake, and all Cairo trembled as the lions roared their approval of their freedom. Then Prince Khumaraweh gave a sign and the lions loped back to their cages.

The Prince was so terrifying that when he went out into the streets of Cairo everyone remained perfectly still and it was said that no dared to sneeze, much less to speak. They watched him pass in silence, and for the rest of the day spoke in whispers.

The Caliph al-Mutadid, the wisest of caliphs in an epoch in decay, surrendered his empire to this grandson of a Turkish slave in return for an annual tribute of 300,000 dinars and the hand of Khumaraweh's beautiful daughter Qatralnada, which means "dewdrop." The tribute and the dowry comprised most of the remaining wealth of Egypt, and thereafter Khumaraweh seems to have lost his popularity in his vast empire which stretched from Libya to the Tigris. In A.D. 896 he was killed in his bed in Damascus by his guards, and when his body was brought back to Cairo in great state to be buried beside his father near the Mosque of Ibn Tulun, it was said that at the moment he was being lowered into his grave the seven Koran readers came to the passage: "Seize ye him and drag him into the mid-fire of Hell."

As you wander through the Mosque of Ibn Tulun, you do not find yourself thinking of the founder of the short-lived Tulunid dynasty or of his brilliant and feverish son. It is as though the mosque grew of its own accord, as though it had been here for everlasting. Those proportions, in their delicacy and strength, are profoundly satisfying, and I think it is because the utmost simplicity is allied to an exact minimum of decoration, like a wave which is all the more beautiful because there is a lacy film of white foam about to break. No doubt the strange corkscrew minaret derives from Samarra, and these pointed arches may not be the earliest ever constructed—that honor appears to belong to the archway in the Nilometer on Rhoda island built by Ibn Tulun fifteen years earlier. Here we see the beginning of the soaring Gothic arch while beside it stands a minaret which derives in straight line of descent from the ziggurats of ancient Babylonia, and they are not incompatible, and are at peace with one another.

In his dedicatory inscription Ibn Tulun described his newly built mosque as "a holy and felicitous place built for the Muhammadan community from the legitimate wealth given to him by God." Here holiness and felicity dwell together, and a quiet splendor. There are more beautiful mosques elsewhere, and in Persia especially you will come upon mosques which flash with shimmering blue and yellow tiles, divinity arrayed in voluptuous garments. But here there are only white walls, a white fountain, and the hovering shadows.

A MUSEUM LIKE A RAILROAD STATION

From time to time wise people find themselves asking the question: "What is a museum? What should it do? Why are all the existing museums with very few exceptions so terribly unsatisfactory?" There are no simple answers. You walk wearily along the marble floors, peering at objects in glass cases, at paintings high on the wall, at statues roped off and with large signs saying: "Do not touch," and there comes a moment when the exhausted feet and the exhausted mind rebel. Something has gone wrong. If a museum is a treasure chest of the most brilliant and beautiful objects from the past, it should be the purest joy to walk through it. Then why is it such a weariness of the mind and the flesh?

I suspect that the museum directors have a good deal to do with it. They have not worked out an intelligible philosophy or an intelligible aesthetics. They have not thought sufficiently about the social function of the museum in the community. They have a passion for sealing everything in glass boxes, and like fashionable window-dressers they amuse themselves with special lighting effects and dramatic presentations of their wares. "Follow me, observe my movements, see how splendidly I have lit these Rembrandts and this Etruscan vase! I have gathered all the past in my embrace, and see how cunningly I have rearranged it for your special delectation." But this is where things go wrong, for it is precisely the cunning, the mounting, the lighting effects, the interminable commentaries that get in the way. Exquisitely self-indulgent, the museum directors *play* with the objects entrusted to their care and are determined

54

to impose themselves upon them. The past becomes the victim of their frivolity.

No one could accuse Auguste Mariette, the great Egyptologist, of frivolity. He built the first museum of Egyptian antiquities at Bulaq near the Cairo railroad station and filled it with the treasures he found during excavations at Thebes, Edfu, Dendera, Abydos and a hundred other places. He was a short, tough, bearded man with a lust for excavations and an absolute determination to build one of the world's great museums. The Egyptians loved him because he was gracious, sensible, and devoted to them. The Khedive made him a Bey and later a Pasha. He became the most powerful European in Egypt and remained completely incorruptible. What he loved most of all was his museum which resembled a vast storage barn where everything was displayed in wonderful disorder. In 1902, twenty years after his death, when the Bulaq museum was bursting at the seams, a new museum near the present Hilton Hotel was built to house the Egyptian treasures. His students, nearly all of them Frenchmen, were still in command. They built in his memory a museum like a railroad station.

What Auguste Mariette wanted and planned for was a building large enough to hold the fruit of a thousand excavations, for he was well aware that Egyptian archaeology was still in its infancy. The statues of Egyptian kings are sometimes twenty feet high, and he wanted a suitable place for them. When you enter the museum today and stand under the dark, forbidding rotunda, you are confronted with vast monolithic creatures gloomily confronting the stray shafts of sunlight that somehow penetrate the darkness and they might all be taken for trains preparing to leave for far-off places. There is a feeling of feverish urgency and disorder. Seti I and Ramses II are getting up steam, Queen Hatshepsut is already on her way to the heavenly fields beyond the western mountains, and Amenhotep III is already leaving the railroad station for a trial run to Thebes. Pistons gleam; the smoke and steam are everywhere; thousands of passengers are hurrying to board the trains.

Nor is it far-fetched to imagine the museum as a railroad station. Those pharaohs were all sleek engines of power, advancing with the momentum of divinity, mechanical and austere. They move with an enviable assurance and never for a moment has it occurred to them that they are not in command of their destiny. But it is their very hugeness, as they crowd under the rotunda, that makes them ultimately unsatisfying. By bringing them all together Mariette and his successors have done them a disservice, for in the end they negate one another. So many towering lumps of granite ultimately become a single lump of granite, and every statue becomes simply one more facet of the gigantic machine of Egyptian dynastic art. What a place it is! A huge, cavernous railroad station made of cast iron, the terminus of four thousand years of Egyptian history.

And what treasures it has! The museum directors have utterly failed to solve the problem of displaying the treasures properly, but it scarcely matters. All that is needed is a roof: the objects can then be set down at random for all the difference it makes! But in their wisdom the directors have selected two rather small, not very prepossessing rooms for their most sumptuous treasures. One is upstairs, the other downstairs. One holds the treasure from Tutankhamen's tomb, the other holds treasures from the age of Akhnaten, including the two colossal statues of the King which show him pot-bellied and weak-chested, with his hands folded across his chest, his face long and lean and full of a fiery intelligence. These two statues are intended to be seen in bright sunlight at a distance of a hundred yards, but in this room you cannot get more than ten yards away from them. They were destroyed by Akhnaten's successors, cut to pieces, and thrown into a well. Now, restored, they possess a springing life, a wonderful urgency, a sense of majesty. The heretical King worshiped the Single Sun, married Princess Nefertiti, and fathered a flock of beautiful daughters. He alone, of all the Pharaohs, seems to charge the air with energy and electricity. He must have possessed stupendous qualities, for almost single-handedly he changed the direction of Egyptian art by insisting that the traditional forms must be abandoned and everything must be seen with fresh eyes; and although after his death the ancient forms returned, his influence can be felt through all the remaining years of Egyptian art. He was the most triumphant of Pharaohs, for although he reigned very briefly and his armies were defeated in the field and the priests rose against him and probably murdered him, and there remains of him nothing but the great art he brought into being, he survives as a living presence while the others perished. That long, angular, pale face with the full lips and the brooding eyes is something to conjure with. There, transported to about the year 1360 B.C., is modern man.

Akhnaten is a comparatively recent discovery, for very little was known about him until about the turn of the century, and the colossal statues were found as recently as 1925. They proved that he had time enough to build his own temple in Karnak before moving his capital to Tell el Amarna far to the north. These statues stood against columns in the portico of a temple dedicated to Aten, the Single Sun, and their presence was a sufficient statement that the new religion of Aten was under the protection of the Pharaoh. No one had ever carved statues like this before: thick thighs, bulbous belly, flat chest, thin stalk-like neck, face like an enormous V with a crown that was topheavy and designed to be far more decorative than the customary Egyptian crowns. These statues were happy caricatures of the reigning Pharaoh; naturalism was thrown to the winds; the essential, the memorable image was made. In the past the Pharaohs had shown themselves impassive and majestic, immensely powerful, moving with the precision of machinery. The fourteen-foot statue of Akhnaten suggests power only by its size: what it expresses most of all is a breathtaking gaiety, as befitted the author of the great *Hymn to the Sun:*

> *Lovely is Thy rising on the horizon of heaven,*
> *O living Aten, Thou who givest life.*
> *Thou risest in the eastern sky,*
> *And all the land is colored with Thy loveliness,*
> *For Thou art splendid, mighty, and beautiful,*
> *Being uplifted over all creation.*
> *Thy rays embrace the earth and everything made by Thee.*
> *Thou art Ra, and all are made subject to Thee*
> *For the sake of the beloved Sun.*
> *Thou art afar off, but Thy rays lie on the earth,*
> *Thou art in the faces of men, and they watch for Thee . . .*

Perhaps five hundred sculptures remain from his reign, but there is only a handful of them in the Egyptian Museum: the lovely head of a princess, a relief showing Akhnaten worshiping the sun, a beautiful portrait of Nefertiti. There are some painted frescoes of birds flying over lotuses, and little more. Yet that single room was more precious to me than the room upstairs flowing with all the gold and jewelry found in Tutankhamen's tomb. The art of Tutankhamen's tomb is already overblown and effete. Only a few years, perhaps eight or nine, separate the death of Akhnaten and the death of Tutankhamen. Now the ancient lumbering machinery of traditional Egyptian art was working again, with here and there some signs of Akhnaten's sense of freedom and daring. In time tradition, like the sands of the desert, would cover everything.

In the museum like a railroad station order breaks down; the huge imperial figures have pride of place; they stand there higgledy-piggledy, glowering confusedly on the mortals hovering below; the Hellenistic sculptures crowd together in a mad, dark muddle. But here and there you come upon rooms where there is a hint of order: there is a small room filled with painted portraits from Coptic coffins, it is well lit, and the faces with the enormous searching eyes are filled with brooding life. But this is not genius; there is no electric shock; no sense of revelation. For this you must return to the small room where Akhnaten stands covered with dust, his strange face towering over the cracked and broken body, a dusty stone beard attached to his jutting jaw, his battered arms folded across his chest, and suddenly he becomes very beautiful as you realize that in that luminous face there shone, very briefly, the hope of a great flowering, a belief in the essential gaiety of all living things under the sun.

JORDAN

THE YOUNG OFFICERS

When Lawrence of Arabia came to Amman in 1921, he found only a small village inhabited largely by Circassians, with one or two government offices. He was then very briefly an administrative officer in charge of bringing order to a country ravaged by war and tribal feuds; and since he had no heart for administrative work and regularly dumped all the papers on his desk into the trash can, he was usually to be found racing across the country by car, or riding the Hedjaz railway, or flying over the country. Amman was just "an emptiness." It had not changed very much since the time forty years earlier when Captain Claude Conder reached Amman and came down "a silent valley, with a clear stream, running over a pebbly bed and flanked here and there with oleanders, while the cows and camels are cropping green turf in the flat meadow between hills utterly bare of tree or shrub." He found some miserable wattle huts belonging to the Circassians, the ruins of Roman houses and tombs, and a ruined mosque on Citadel Hill. There were so many Roman ruins that he imagined he had come upon the best or nearly the best of Roman cities in the Middle East.

Today, except for the great amphitheatre which has been completely excavated, it would be very difficult to find the Roman city and just as difficult to find the clear stream running over the pebbly bed. The old Amman of the Circassians has vanished, and the present capital of the Hashemite Kingdom of Jordan is a bustling modern city with skyscraper hotels, air pollution, traffic jams, universities, nightclubs, and a dubious plumbing system. Traffic is fast and furious, and corners are turned on two wheels. All the seven hills of Amman are crowded with houses, and the city is beginning to spill over into the desert.

There should be a universal law against building cities on seven hills. One hill is usually sufficient; two hills provide a nice balance; seven hills are very nearly unmanageable. The ancient Ammonites solved the problem neatly by establishing their main fortifications on Citadel Hill and leaving the other hills to be defended as best they could. They called their city Rabbath Ammon, or "Great Ammon," and they appear to have been a quarrelsome and warlike people. They first appear in history as victors in a war against Bashan, carrying off as a trophy King Og's iron bed, which was more than sixteen feet long and seven feet broad. Many years later King David attacked the city and conquered it, taking "exceedingly much spoil" and massacring the inhabitants in various fearful ways recorded in the second *Book of Samuel:* "And he brought forth the people that were therein, and put them under saws, and under harrows of iron, and under axes of iron, and made them pass through the brick-kiln." By this last punishment it was meant that they were burned alive. David also took possession of the crown of the King of Rabbath Ammon, which weighed one talent of gold and was set with jewels.

Nevertheless Ammon survived as an independent state, and we hear of another King of Ammon supplying David with provisions during his war against Absalom. These provisions consisted of "beds and basons," but something has evidently gone wrong in the text. The iron bed of Og, as a war trophy, is credible, but "beds and basons" as instruments of war defy credibility. Solomon, in an effort to pacify the tribes, elevated a shrine to Milcom, the god of the Ammonites, in a high place in Jerusalem, but under King Josiah the shrine was torn down and the grove of trees around it was cut down. Bones were strewn over the place, and from being a shrine it became a charnel yard.

Of the ancient kingdom of Ammon nothing remains except the ruins of some hilltop forts, some bronze daggers and arrowheads, a few scarabs and seals, and some fragments of scale armor. But if there is little to remind us of the biblical age, there is in the Jordan Archaeological Museum a startling reminder of the art of portraiture going back to the Neolithic Age (7000–4500 B.C.). To revive the dead, to bring them back into recognizable form, Neolithic sculptors molded plaster over human skulls and placed shells in the eye-sockets. The plaster followed the features of the dead man, with the result that we know their exact appearance. Nothing quite like this has been found in any other culture, and those heads, though they consist of nothing more than plaster wrapped around a skull, are the first human portraits.

The Archaeological Museum in Amman is a rather haphazard affair, well lit but not very well arranged, with Neolithic, Bronze Age, Greek, Roman, Ghassanid, and Islamic objects cheek by jowl. The most memorable statue is a Hellenistic Apollo crowned with laurel leaves, the body modeled with the assurance of a great master, at once delicate and strong, the head bowed in thought, and there is about that head, made heavy by the presence of the crown of leaves that weighs against his temples, an extraordinary gravity, so that the youthful, nubile body seems scarcely able to support it. It is like a presage of those heavy-headed divinities of India that mysteriously transform stone into pure thought.

It is worth pausing before this Apollo, which must have been carved for a temple to Apollo built by Ptolemy II Philadelphus in the third century B.C. when he rebuilt Amman and called it Philadelphia after his own name. The nose has been broken, a forearm and a hand are missing. Here and there we see marble supports which show that it is not yet in its completely finished state, has not yet left the sculptor's studio. But it will need only a few hours' work to bring it to completion, and so we have the statue when it was still in the possession of the sculptor, before it was ever exhibited publicly. The more one looks at the sculpture, the more it appears to possess a personal and intimate character. Here is Apollo in his youthful glory, but here is also the youthful model for whom the sculptor possessed a brooding affection. Divine Apollo with his five-fold crown of laurels reflects an unknown sculptor's human passion.

Apollo and the plastered Neolithic heads were sufficient excuse for haunting the museum on Citadel Hill, where there was also a ruined temple to Hercules which reputedly housed a thirty-foot statue of the god, and some Roman walls of little more interest than a child's discarded toys. The truth was that there was very little to see in Amman, and once you had driven up and down the seven hills there was very little left to do. I wanted to go to a place called Azraq of the Pools. There were delays. I could not find a driver. While waiting for the perfect driver to appear, I fell in with some young officers at the riding club. In retrospect I realize

I must have been in a state of absolute boredom, for I had not the slightest interest in young officers or in riding. Nevertheless in Amman it seemed to make sense.

These young officers were, I suppose, the flower of the Jordanian army. They were so sleek, so handsome, so elegant that they might have stepped out of the pages of a fashion magazine. They rode superbly. They talked with a delightful singsong accent in English and French. Many of them had long, narrow, aristocratic faces and pencil thin mustaches, and they adored horses and women. It appeared that they were the *jeunesse dorée* of Amman and believed the city was created for their own enjoyment. But since the stables and the clubhouse were some distance from the city, they were perfectly content to abandon the city to its fate in their admiration for their horses.

"Of course we're all ruining ourselves!" the most elegant one said. "A horse and its upkeep are terribly expensive. I'm up to my eyes in debt with not the slightest hope of paying off my creditors. Not betting, mind you! I've never betted in my life! Just the horses cost a fortune!"

"How many horses have you got?"

"Five! That's the bare minimum. If you don't have five horses, life is not worth living! I tell you, God gave nothing more noble to a man than a horse! If I had to choose between my horses and my mistresses, I would choose the horses every time!"

He leaned back in the comfortable red leather armchair, glanced up at the silver trophies on the wall, ordered another whiskey, stroked his curling mustache, and said with the air of someone who has found the truth and is prepared to announce it with conviction: "The truth is that we come to life only when we are on horseback or on camels. We belong to the desert, not to the cities, not to machinery, not to modern life. Of course we can catch up. We can make machines, if we have to, but at the end of the day we'll come home and ride a horse. Ultimately the modern world means absolutely nothing to us!"

Obviously it meant a good deal to him, for he enjoyed his comforts, but at the core of him there was an anarchic horror of the modern world which placed him in a straitjacket and squeezed the life out of him. He wanted the freedom of the desert and hated every hour he spent in his office. He was an artillery captain, and it appeared that captains were continually being drowned in paperwork.

Charles Doughty, the English traveler and poet, once wrote: "Truly there is nearly no Arab who durst descend alone into the tribe, and set his face to contradict the multitude." I wanted to find out more about the Arab mind. Was it true that the Arabs were still essentially tribal, acquiescent to whatever demands were made by their chieftains, aware of the tribe more than of the nation, caught up in the demanding consciousness of the tribe, and at its mercy?

He said: "All Arabs are rebellious, for every Arab wants to be the chief of his tribe. But what is the tribe? My tribe is the Army. I have another tribe—my friends in the riding club. My father is one of the King's ministers—another tribe. My family comes from Jerash—another tribe. So many tribes! And then, larger than any of these tribes, is the realm of Islam with Muhammad as the Prophet King! To all these tribes I owe my loyalty."

"And when they conflict?"

"When they conflict, I owe my loyalty to Allah and to the Prophet."

A little while later, when we were talking about Middle Eastern politics, he said: "We do not talk about the Jews. They do not exist."

"How can you say that since it is undoubtedly true that they existed, do exist, and will continue to exist?"

We argued and got nowhere. That the Jews do not exist was so firmly planted in his mind that it was ineradicable. He did not mean that he refused to think about them; he meant that they had no existence, no reality except perhaps as points of danger. There was a map on the wall. Israel was not marked on the map. Instead there were the ominous words: OCCUPIED TERRITORY. Occupied by whom?

He did mention the Jews a little later, for he said: "I'll probably be killed in a war against the Jews, and my creditors will go mad." Then he laughed and went on to talk about his horses.

He was a kindly man, and if he was bigoted, it was a bigotry he shared with every Jordanian I met. I could not change it. I told him I could not find a good driver to take me to Azraq. He said: "I'll find you one," and he was as good as his word.

PETRA

Abdul Razak was a Bedouin who wore his *keffiyah* rakishly, laughed a good deal and smiled frequently. He had a rather square face, beetling eyebrows, a jutting chin, and the body of a young wrestler. One morning in Amman he handed me a piece of paper signed by the young artillery captain at the riding club. It read: "Here is your man. You will like him. He will take you wherever you want to go." This was not quite true. I went wherever Abdul Razak wanted to go.

He said: "You want to leave now? Very good. We are going to Petra."

"I want to go to Azraq."

"Why?"

"Why not? I want to go there."

He looked at me pityingly.

"Petra is better," he announced firmly. "It is a good day to go to Petra."

"I want to go to Azraq. We'll go to Petra some other day."

"No, Petra is better."

So we went to Petra along the Desert Highway, while he talked encouragingly about all the marvelous things I would see there. He was born in the village of Elji which faces the narrow entrance into the long-dead city. He liked talking, talked well, and sometimes consulted a well-thumbed pocket dictionary. I wished he would not consult the dictionary so often because it meant that he took both hands off the wheel. He said "afficient" when he meant "efficient," and he especially liked long, large-sounding words like "stupiferous" and "magnimonous" and "splendiderous." Most of his new-found words were improvements on the originals.

What was chiefly remarkable about Abdul Razak was a kind of openness, a way of looking at the world which was at once very mature and almost childlike. He could not have been more than twenty-three or twenty-four, but he sometimes talked like an old man. Once he said: "I talk too much. I have no secrets. I must therefore invent a secret, but this is difficult. Will you help me to invent a secret?" He laughed, raised his hands high above the wheel, and then brought them back with a resounding crash so that the automobile fairly jumped, while I thought that the Arabs were in love with secrets and there cannot be many who do not hoard a nest of them.

The Arab mind? Sensualists, mathematicians, wanderers without roots, anchored in the desert and restless in cities. The pictorial imagination was linear: hence the beauty and elegance of Kufic script and the rejection of images of the human body as something not worth depicting. I thought of Ibn al-Arabi, the twelfth-century mystic, who wrote that he was closer to God in the arms of a woman than anywhere else, and of al-Hallaj, who lived in Baghdad in the tenth century, and wrote: "If the sun should rise at night, the dawn of hearts would have no setting." Al-Hallaj once stretched out his hand and drew an apple from an invisible tree, and when someone observed that the apple was full of maggot holes, he said: "How could it be otherwise? I plucked the apple from a tree in the Mansion of Eternity and brought it into the House of Decay, and that is why it is touched with corruption!" And there was another quality in the Arab mind which I could only call mischievousness, the delight in play of a faintly malicious character, and those interminable arguments around a fixed point which were essentially verbal games intended to sharpen the wits.

"You know very well you terrify me when you keep your hands off the wheel," I said. "With a camel it doesn't matter very much whether you hold onto the reins, but with a car it is different."

"Terrifying a friend is a sign of friendship," he said, and it was one more clue to the Arab character.

It was a dazzling day under the enormous cloudless sky, and the desert stretching away on both sides of the Desert Highway. There was little traffic along the road, and sometimes I thought I could make out the ancient Roman road, built by the Emperor Trajan, which ran from

Damascus to Aila on the Gulf of Aqaba, and occasionally we saw the small black trains of the Hedjaz Railway which Lawrence of Arabia had attacked during the desert war against the Turks. From the road they looked so improbably small and spewed out such improbable balloons of black smoke that I began to think they were not real trains at all but toy trains constructed for the delectation of passengers along the highway.

It appeared that Abdul Razak had good and excellent reasons for wanting to go to Petra. A wedding in the family was about to take place, he had not seen his favorite brother for over a year, and someone in Petra owed him fifty dollars. He explained that the family had a house at Elji. "It is all yours," he said, and went on to enumerate the eight or nine people who lived in the four-room house.

"Mine?" I asked.

"They'll all be very nice to you and wait on you and make you comfortable," he laughed. "I will tell them you are my friend and they will treat you like a king—better than a king."

We reached Maan, which I had imagined to be a large and thriving town, because it was the administrative center of all southern Jordan, and found it to be little more than a mud-brick village with a railroad station, and some sand-blown acacia trees. Camels, donkeys, and scavenger dogs wander through the hot sand, and there were small booths where men sat within the ample folds of their gowns, sipped tea, argued, flung out their hands in explosive gestures, or fingered their bright worry-beads which are designed precisely for the purpose of preventing them from making explosive gestures. Only a few women appeared, draped in black and heavy with jewelry. Maan lay dozing in the sun, the sudden arrival of the train giving it a sudden jolt as all eyes turned toward the railroad station. We had seen the toy train from the Desert Highway; now it had grown to full size, for the desert, like the sea, changes all proportions and narrows all distances.

Petra lies north of Maan. We turned west and then north until the land changed from rolling plains of sand to pitiless sandstone mountains. Abdul Razak dropped me outside a vast columned Nabataean tomb converted into a rest-house, waved in the direction of the narrow slit through the mountains that led to Petra, and sped off in the direction of Elji to see his brother and to collect fifty dollars from a cousin.

The rest-house was comfortable, austere, expensive, and more elegant than most tombs. In fact the tomb contained the dining room and the offices, while the bedrooms were built around it, offering a wonderful view of a wild valley. There were other smaller tombs carved into the rock. In one of these caves Johann Ludwig Burckhardt, the Swiss traveler and orientalist, camped before riding down to the slit in the mountains surrounding Petra, thus becoming the first European for more than six hundred years to enter the forgotten city. He came disguised as a Moslem, assuming the name of Ibrahim ibn Abdullah, and every moment of his journey he was in great danger.

The modern traveler is in no danger at all. Pack mules and horses are waiting to take him to Petra; a wooden office issues tickets; policemen regulate the traffic. "The rose-red city half as old as time" is subject to governmental restrictions; there are notices in English and Arabic telling you what you must and must not do. You tell yourself that the romance has departed and it is absurd to have an office issuing tickets to permit you to visit Petra. As well apply to an office for permission to dream! But the country must have revenue, the slit can be guarded by a single man with a rifle, and in any case the ticket costs the equivalent of thirty cents and the Bedouin enter free. Petra has entered the twentieth century.

The Arab boys are shouting and hustling, the horses are neighing, and there is the clack and slither of hooves on shining rocks rounded and smoothed by fierce winter winds. Bargaining, shouting, the usual uproar of the Arab market place. At last, seduced by the smile of a fresh-faced ten-year-old, I found a dappled mare who looked capable of making a long journey at a reasonable pace, steady and reliable, with the wisdom of old age. I should have known better. She was very frisky.

The slit, called the *syq* by the Arabs, is about a mile and a half long, dank, gloomy, in perpetual twilight. There are many turns in this narrow cleft, which resembles a road tortuously groping its way through the mountain. The rocky walls seem to meet overhead, but occasionally there is a patch of yellow high above; and there are wild fig trees with crawling roots and clumps of pink oleander growing in the cracks; and the smell of vegetation after the smell of the sand and of the scalded rocks. Along one side there is a channel cut into the foot of the rocks, which once carried water from Wadi Musa into the secret city. The strangest thing of all is the silence of the place broken only by the scurrying of stones under the horses' hoofs and the occasional voice of an Arab boy speaking to one of the horses as he runs beside it. Sometimes, too, there came the soughing of the wind among the oleanders at the top of the cliffs.

And this dark road twisting and turning unaccountably has the curious effect of lulling the senses so that you have absolutely no sense of expectancy. You are going through a tunnel where the walls are carved and broken like the rocks in Sesshu's paintings, faintly sinister, and it is impossible to see the path ahead for more than a few feet. If it was not for the smiling long-gowned Arab boy talking to the horse, you would feel hopelessly lost. The *syq* is a prison in which you are permitted to ride lugubriously from one dark cave to the next. Gothic horrors would find an appropriate setting in the *syq*.

And suddenly, startlingly, just at the moment when you are beginning to think the rock tunnel is your natural home, and that there is no escape, there appears, at the last turning of the road, a flash of purest red in the form of a temple carved in rock, with the columns set against the rich green of oleanders. The temple is carved in soft sandstone deeply weathered, pitted and pockmarked with bullet-holes, but at first glance it looks wonderfully fresh and new. In that enchanted moment when you escape from a tunnel a mile and a half long, you see a temple of perfect proportions and immaculate beauty, glowing like a bonfire in the hot sun.

There is no mistaking the intention of the builders—to shock, to assert, to demonstrate the most magnificent art, here, at this precise point where the tunnel ends. This is the place of honor; it is the salute as you enter the great painted bowl of Petra, and it whets your appetite for more. Unfortunately there is no other building in the whole of Petra which compares with it.

The Arabs call it the Kazneh, or Treasury. No gold has been found in the treasury, which was almost certainly the tomb of a Nabataean king. With the help of the imagination it is possible to make out some of the carvings—on the lower ground there appears to be a horseman charged by two serpents; winged griffons and chalices on the architrave; the goddess Isis armed with her cornucopeia above. The scale is prodigious, for the door leading into the tomb is forty feet high, and people standing under the colonnade look like midgets. The Kazneh is essentially Hellenistic in its proportions, its grace, and its refinement, and dates from about 200 B.C.

A little way beyond the Kazneh we see the ancient city of Petra, all ruins now, with rock tombs on all the surrounding cliffs and rocky outcrops. The pitiable remnants of a Roman triumphal archway, a few stones, being all that is left of a Crusader castle, and always the tombs carved in the rock. But it is not for these things that one goes to Petra. One goes to see the mountains, which are rainbow colored, all red and blue and green and yellow in lusty stripes, all aflame with the colors left by an ancient volcanic explosion, so that these mountains appear to be in perpetual movement, spinning round and round, making you dizzy.

Scarcely anything is left of the ancient city: rubble, rock-hewn steps, foundations of palaces and temples long since swept away, tombs like stepping stones climbing up the sides of mountains, and sometimes the rock has weathered in such a way that it gives the appearance of being still molten, of having been poured over the tomb, of wrapping itself round the tomb like folds of cloth. Sometimes the stairways climb the mountain and then cease, as though they had changed their mind and wanted to go no further. There is a sense of aimlessness, as though it was all a backdrop for a play that had not yet been written, although in fact the play was written long ago and only the fiery backdrop remained.

The mare was skittish and decided to race across the rubble plain toward the black tents of some Bedouin camped below a tomb three stories high, with a great array of columns carved in the rock, clearly imitating the facade of a palace. The Bedouin looked poor and bedraggled, they clustered round the mare, shouted for baksheesh, displayed long knives, and were up to mischief. The Arab boy with the engaging smile arrived in time to prevent the highway robbery, waving his small arms and bawling at the top of his voice until the knives were put away.

We rode off toward the small museum, which was another tomb carved out of the rock and reached by a smooth and slippery stairway. Inside the museum there were a few Nabataean plates decorated with leaves and some sculptures so battered that it was impossible to recognize whether they were male or female. From the steps of the museum, looking out at the vast valley and the painted mountains in the pure air, it was easy to imagine a splendid city with palaces and law-courts and market-places, where now there was only rubble and the campfires of the Bedouin.

THE NABATAEANS

Even today, though the scholars have raked over their ruins for a century and copied out all the surviving fragments of their writing, the Nabataeans remain strangely elusive. Like all people who leave no literature, they wear their silence uncomfortably. We have no songs, no hymns, no histories, and we scarcely know what they looked like, for we have only the occasional portraits of their later kings stamped on coins and the shadowy portraits of their gods. The few surviving documents written on papyrus deal with commercial transactions and tell us no more than we knew before: that they were traders. We know them by their tombs, the buildings they carved out of rock, their frail pottery and the great cisterns they carved in the desert, determined to make it flower. Grain, fruit and vegetables grew at their bidding in deserts now featureless and empty. They built ships, possessed their own temples in all the seaports of the eastern Mediterranean, traded with Africa and India, and converted the Red Sea into their private lake. For a brief period between the first centuries B.C. and A.D. the Nabataean kingdom rose to spectacular power and wealth. Then abruptly it vanished. The descendants of these traders and conquerors are the Howeitat Arabs whose black tents stand out against the desert. A few of the Howeitat still live in the huddled caves of Petra.

What little we know about the ancient history of the Nabataeans comes from the two Greek historians Diodorus Siculus and Strabo, who wrote during the age of Augustus at a time when the kingdom had reached its greatest extent, including even Damascus within its boundaries. Yet the two historians both wrote about the Nabataeans as though from an immense distance, never quite bringing them into focus, as though they had read about them in old books and filled up the gaps with legend and hearsay and pure inventions. Diodorus Siculus, for example, tells us that they had a law "neither to sow corn nor to plant any fruit-bearing trees nor to use wine nor to build houses," and we know that they did all these things.

He tells an entertaining story about their battles with Antigonus, Alexander the Great's successor as king of Syria. When the young men were absent at a great fair somewhere in the neighborhood, Antigonus launched a surprise attack on Petra, killed most of the old men, women and children, and hurriedly retreated with an immense booty of frankincense and myrrh and five hundred talents of silver. Soon the young men returned, surveyed the damage, and went off in pursuit of the Greeks. Antigonus was so sure that he would not be pursued that he took no precautions. His army was encamped in the desert when the Nabataeans suddenly attacked and sacked the camp. About four thousand Greeks were massacred, and only fifty, including Antigonus, got away. It was an overwhelming defeat, but the Nabataeans were sensible people accustomed to counting the profit and loss, and they knew that Antigonus commanded powerful forces in the north. Accordingly they wrote a letter, explaining that they had been distressed at discovering their dead in Petra and had perhaps been more destructive than the situation demanded; they offered friendship. Antigonus replied in similar terms, and proceeded to gather an army strong enough to destroy the Nabataeans to the last man. Once again the Greek army marched south. This time the Nabataeans were forewarned, and when the Greeks under Demetrius reached Petra, the Nabataeans simply dispersed into the desert. Demetrius failed to storm the Rock, and would have returned home empty-handed if an embassy had not arrived from the Nabataean king offering costly presents. In this way, like good traders, the Nabataeans sought to make the enemy's losses profitable.

These battles and forays took place about 312 B.C. For nearly three hundred years we hear little more about the Nabataeans. In 47 B.C. Julius Caesar called upon their king Malek I to provide him with cavalry for his Alexandrian wars. Thereafter, as we might expect, the Nabataeans come more and more within the Roman sphere of influence, but knowledge of them remained curiously sketchy. When Strabo wished to describe the character of the Nabataeans, he consulted Ahenodorus, the friend and tutor of the Emperor Augustus. Ahenodorus was born in Petra, he was a scholar and a cultivated member of the court, and he might be expected to discourse on the Nabataean character with accuracy and understanding. So perhaps he did, but as Strabo records the conversation, we have the feeling that his attention sometimes wavered. The Nabataeans, as he describes them in the only lengthy discussion which has survived from antiquity, retain an aura of mystery and legend. The description should be quoted in full because it is oddly convincing and at the same time very nearly incredible. Here is Strabo's description of the Nabataeans as it was related to him by Ahenodorus:

> These people are intelligent and industrious, with a fondness for owning property, so much so that those who diminish their property are publicly penalized, while those who increase their property receive public honors. They have few slaves, and therefore must be waited upon by their relatives or by each other, or they do their own chores; and the custom extends even to their kings. They take their meals in common, with thirteen men sitting at table attended by two singing girls. The king in his palace offers many magnificent banquets, but no one drinks more than eleven cups of wine, always using a different golden cup. The king is so democratic that in addition to serving himself he sometimes serves his guests. He often renders an account of his kingship to the popular assembly, and sometimes also the conduct of his life is examined. Their dwellings are built of great blocks of stonework, but their cities are unwalled because of the prevailing peace.
>
> Over most of the country there are extensive orchards, but there are no olive fields. They use sesame oil instead. Their sheep have white fleeces, and the oxen are large. The country produces no horses, camels performing the service which horses perform in other countries. The people go without tunics, but wear girdles about their waists and they have slippers on their feet—even the kings wear slippers, but theirs are purple.
>
> Many things are imported from other countries, but in some cases we also manufacture the same things we import, as for example gold and silver and most of the aromatics, but we produce no brass or iron, nor purple cloth, nor styrax, crocus, costaria, embossed work, paintings and mouldings.
>
> The Nabataeans have the same regard for the dead as for dung; as Heracleitus says, dead bodies are more fit to be thrown away than dung.

They worship the sun, setting up an altar on top of the house and pouring libations on it daily and burning frankincense.

Such was the verdict of a charming and sophisticated Nabataean on his own countrymen as it filtered down through the mind of Strabo. Some of it is untrue. The rock tombs at Petra speak of a profound veneration for the dead, and to say that their cities were unwalled is to pay insufficient attention to the fact that they had only one city of any size, and that was Petra, which was walled by mountains. Nor is it likely that the Nabataeans went about nearly naked, wearing only girdles about their waists, for the hot sun and the bitterly cold nights demanded the wearing of clothes.

So we are left with the sketchiest picture of the Nabataeans, who came out of the desert, conquered the Edomites, captured Petra, made it their capital, and demanded tribute from every caravan passing nearby, growing rich by taxing the spice and incense caravans from the Hadhramaut. We know them best from their gods: Hadad the Thunder-bearer, lord of the worlds; Atargatis, goddess of fertility, who appears as a mermaid or as a woman wearing a crown of fishes; and Dushara, lord of the mountains, who was represented by a pillar of stone or an obelisk. We know them too from their delicate pottery, as thin as porcelain, with their unsophisticated designs. Of the people themselves and their appearance we know scarcely anything at all. Their greatest contribution to the world was a curiously elongated Arabic script which eventually became stylized into Kufic. In this way they built the bridge from Aramaic to Arabic letters.

For a brief while the Nabataean empire stretched from the Gulf of Aqaba to Damascus and beyond; and Roman seaports saw Nabataean sailors, for we find them building a temple to Hadad at Puteoli near Naples and there are more temples scattered around the Mediterranean. Then came changing trade routes, the rise of Palmyra, the crumbling of Roman power, quarrels among the Arab tribes, and the empire faded. In the third century A.D. there was almost nothing left. The Byzantines came, Islam swept across all this territory, the Crusaders built a fortress at Petra, and surrendered it to Saladin, and then it was forgotten. Through the once busy streets of colored stone wild beasts stalked their prey, and for centuries the Bedouin took shelter in the tombs, leaving no traces of themselves. Petra, forgotten and abandoned, became what it had always been: a vast painted bowl under the open sky.

A JOURNEY TO BEIDHA

Early one morning, in the pure freshness of the dawn, with the wind running and the sky the color of amethysts, pale and sparkling, we set out for Beidha, which is only some seven or eight miles from Petra as the crow flies, but eleven or twelve miles to the traveler on horseback. There is no road, only a rarely traveled lunar landscape which would sometimes, as though to remind us of the world we had abandoned, open out into small desolate fields of springing grass; and then the rocks would close in on us, and we were once more in the lunar landscape, remote from the world.

In the early morning the cool wind blew against our faces, but not for long. As soon as we left the valley and the green slopes of Wadi Musa, the heat began trickling from the sky. At first it came in small scalding drops and then in torrents; the heavens were on fire, and the earth reflected the fire, beating up against our faces, so that we stopped at shorter and shorter intervals to drink the water from Ali Auda's flask. He was a rather small man, quick and trim, with a little tuft of black beard, no more than a few carefully trimmed hairs, and he had high cheekbones and very dark eyes, which seemed always to be in a hurry, for he watched everything. He wore a black and white *keffiyah,* a long gown of checkered brown cotton, and a well-cut coat, which he had bought recently in Maan. He was a hunter, and he had the hunter's desire to merge into the shadows. He had been hired, together with the boy Musa Attiyeh, to take me to Beidha. A policeman, Ibrahim Mahmud, accompanied us. I rode on a white stallion, Ibrahim Mahmud rode on a chestnut mare, and the others walked.

At Petra there was a good deal of shaking of heads when I announced that I was going to Beidha. They said there were few people who knew the road, bandits had been seen there recently, and there was nothing of any interest except some prehistoric ruins. I had discussed Beidha with Dr. Kathleen Kenyon, the archaeologist, and she too had expressed the opinion that the journey was profitless, the ruins not worth examining. But Edward Palmer, one of the greatest of nineteenth-century explorers, had thought it worth his trouble to make the journey in the company of tribesmen who staged a mutiny when he arrived there, and Charles Doughty, a still greater explorer, had thought wistfully of going there, but was dissuaded on the grounds of the danger and difficulty of the journey. But the warring tribes of Bedouin had long since been rounded up by the desert patrols, and today there is no danger.

Although there was no danger, there was excitement: the excitement of seeing that lunar landscape unfolding in massive hills of glaring limestone, the earth turned white and savage, the naked mountains all torn and twisted, the energy still in them. It was a landscape in convulsions. We rode slowly, and I would find myself lowering my eyes to study the blue beads knitted into the stallion's mane, and then looking up, wondering whether those mountains would still be standing there, so dream-like and improbable they were.

There were no roads, no field tracks, no pathways. We skirted the edges of cliffs with thousand-foot drops, clambered over the round and pitted rocks, and scurried along the ridges of the limestone mountains, the stallion treading delicately. Sometimes there were huge humps of rock worn so smooth that even that sure-footed stallion could not clamber up them with a rider, and so I had to dismount. Dismounting presented difficulties. I had torn a muscle in my leg, and I could no more have climbed over those smooth humps of rock than reached over and touched the mountains in the distance. Ali Auda solved the problem with ease, by carrying me on his back. He was small but powerfully built, and very agile. He simply lifted me on his back as though I were a child, and crouching low, he went running up the smooth rock like a young panther.

We passed Nabataean rock tombs, which looked out of place in this wilderness: in Petra they are close together, or at least within hailing distance of one another, but here they were scattered far and wide. On a ridge just below us there stood the ruins of a Crusader fortress, still elegant, though the tower had fallen in and half the walls had perished.

Ali Auda knew the fortress well, and he could remember the time thirty years ago when the great bell still rang eerily in the high winds of winter. Then abruptly the bell ceased ringing. He thought some shepherds must have taken it away to sell for metal.

"It was a big bell," he said, and he threw his arms wide open to suggest its size. "I don't know how they took it away." He shook his head in bewilderment. "Everything about the castle is big. The Frengies knew what they were up to—they made it impregnable. There wasn't any way men could have captured the castle, and there was no lack of water, for they had six huge cisterns for catching rain-water."

This fortress had once controlled all the trade passing through Petra, but now it was dissolving into its elements. Once there were spices, carpets and fabrics piled high in its cellars, and the knights grew rich on the fees paid by travelers. It was the southernmost of all the Crusader castles, and only the most daring knights could have been chosen for duty in this southern outpost. But of the history of the fortress almost nothing is known.

We know far more about the small stone sanctuary standing high up on the summit of Mount Hor, which could be seen far away across the lunar landscape. On the very tip of the mountain there could be seen the white sanctuary where Aaron was buried according to the command delivered to Moses: "Take Aaron and Eleazar his son, and bring them up unto Mount Hor, and strip Aaron of his garments and put them upon Eleazar his son: and Aaron shall be gathered unto his people, and shall die there." There was something heroic about the aspect of the mountain, so heavy, so domineering, with its powerful shoulders, so that it had something of the appearance of a king looking down on a dead land. Mount Hor was magnificently present, though, as we turned and twisted on the rocky road to Beidha, it seemed to be constantly changing its position.

The summit looked unreachable, but in fact many people have climbed it. Indeed every year in September there is a festival said to take place on the anniversary of Aaron's death; the Muslims have a special reverence for Aaron, whom they call Harun; they climb the mountain, slaughter a sheep and offer prayers for his soul; and there are some who say that it is not Aaron but a Byzantine saint who is buried there. Ali Auda scoffed at such stories, saying that not a single Frengie had ever climbed the mountain, though some had attempted it. When the Frengies were close to the sanctuary they always heard a mysterious voice saying: "Go no further!" and they always turned back.

I asked him whether he had been there, and he said he had been there many times and was never turned back. But once you were on the summit there was nothing to see except a white dome over the tomb and the bones of long-dead sheep, and the way down was worse than the way up.

Twice the path vanished among smooth sloping boulders and twice he carried me on his shoulders. The second time my stallion balked at the smooth rock after pawing it tentatively, and Ali Auda braced himself and as much as carried the stallion up, getting underneath it and lifting it, and then when it was half across he pushed against its rump. When it was over, he wrung the sweat out of his black and white *keffiyah* and said he hoped this was the last time he would have to carry a horse on his back.

The rocks came to an end and suddenly we were in another landscape altogether: thick waving green grass, carob trees, an ancient Roman wall, an air of luxuriance. Here there were springs and twenty acres of land that could be farmed. There was even a pathway leading to some excavations, for the archaeologists had been at work on an early Neolithic settlement, and over five seasons they had left heavy tracks through the grass.

The Neolithic settlement lay in the shadow of Mount Seir, in a wide valley surrounded by limestone cliffs. A maze of small rooms, low walls, stairways, stunted stone pillars and worked stones was all that remained of the settlement that flourished about 8,000 B.C., when stone tools were used but pottery was not yet being made. The excavations lay open to the sky, and on the other side of the valley blue tarpaulins were spread out over the archaeologists' supplies. There was no need to guard the site. Seven or eight months would pass before the archaeologists returned to resume their digging.

I had never seen a Neolithic site before and was fascinated by the smallness of those rooms. It appeared that Neolithic man was about four feet seven inches tall. Their bones have been discovered, the long bones carefully placed together, the rib-cage on one side, the finger bones in a little pile. There were no skulls; possibly they were stored elsewhere. The bones were assembled neatly, according to size. They were an orderly people, who built solidly, raised wheat and barley, kept goats, hunted aurochs, gazelles, wild boars, jackals and hares, and knew where to find flint pebbles, granite, basalt, obsidian, and limestone. All these could be found in the vicinity, but the nearest source of obsidian was in Asia Minor. Oak, juniper and pistachio trees gave them nourishment and heat, and the obsidian spearheads gave them meat. Diana Kirkbride, who superintended the excavations, described in her report rooms which were essentially workrooms as distinguished from living rooms: division of labor had already come into existence.

There were these excavations low to the earth, so low that you might pass them without realizing that an old civilization was being unearthed, and above them hung the beautifully shaped crags like charging elephants, and it was very quiet in this enclosed valley. Here, although the sky was on fire, there was at least the illusion that life was endurable, and my white stallion, grazing on the long grass in the shadow of the rocks, looked as though he might have been there from everlasting.

These Neolithic tribesmen had chosen their site well, for this valley could be well defended. Marauding animals could be easily trapped; advancing enemies could be easily observed. They had found a small paradise.

The white stallion, called Solomon the Magnificent, thought the same, and was too busy grazing to want to be mounted, and cantered off to another part of the valley as soon as he saw me coming. For ten minutes he played this game, and then relented, for his belly was full. He was a noble beast with ropes of turquoise looped in his mane, his saddlecloth crimson, and there were colored stones knotted in his reins. We went on, one valley opening into another, until we reached the syk at Beidha, where Solomon pranced about, so happy he was to contemplate those enormously long grasses and ferns in the shade of the overhanging rocks.

This was another defile, a hundred and fifty feet long and perhaps thirty feet wide. Then there came a small valley twenty yards wide with rocks on either side, and tombs carved in them. Rarely visited and little known, less spectacular than Petra, and much smaller, it was nevertheless an enchanted place. A knife had come down and split the immense blue-grey rock wide open, and through this gap I rode in awed silence, like one who has entered the world of the dead. There was a solemnity about the place which came from its wildness, its abandonment, its shadowiness, for little light filtered down. Among these carved rocks there was peace but no magnificence, only the deep luxurious calm and the sound of waters.

The rock tombs were carved deeply, and the largest of them, with three detached columns, was apparently never completed, for one of the columns was rough-hewn and square, while the others were delicately rounded, supple and strong. In the blue submarine light of the place the world seemed to come to an end in the rustling of grasses and oleanders. Ali Auda was saying pleasantly that once there was a large and thriving city here, but when the city dwellers were attacked they simply abandoned it, opened a door in the rock leading down to a rich and fertile land beneath the surface of the earth, and closed the door behind them.

It was a magical place, and not only for its quietness and remoteness and the legends told about it. There was a sense of intimacy with the long-dead past, a brooding contentment, and at the same time the feeling that a revelation was at hand. Those tombs carved out of the living rock were mouths about to speak and to warn. At Petra, once you have passed through the long winding corridor, you find the city wide open to the sky, the huge painted rocks at play, the scenery so improbable that it becomes enjoyable. The colors shout, and Petra is a theatre. But here, at Beidha, there were no fierce colors, and there is a deep solemnity. You have come to the world's end. Here all that was superfluous has been swept away and there remain only the rocks, the carved columns and the wild grasses.

I had thought that Beidha would be another Petra, smaller perhaps and daintier, and had not expected to find perfection in a cleft in the rock. Almost Beidha was an act of pure meditation. At the world's end the shadow of a fern on the rock was the purest happiness.

We returned to Petra while the heat still roared out of the sky. Ali Auda, having rested at Beidha, was jauntier than ever. He ran low to the ground, moving incredibly fast, darting across that wild landscape with practiced ease. What he was after was the *houbara*, a bird a little like a turkey, nearly extinct now, with a white and creamy flesh. Shots rang out, echoing across the valleys from rock to rock, and then we would see him standing on a crag in the distance, empty handed.

Once again we passed through a Neolithic village, saw Mount Hor with Aaron's tomb in the distance, looked down on a Roman wall and a Crusader castle, the centuries flashing past in a landscape as violent as dreams. The rocks had not yet hardened; they were still molten. The blue tents and tarpaulins of Miss Kirkbride's archaeological expedition were still where she left them, neatly folded, with stones to weigh them down, and Ali Auda was still running up and down the bare scalding rocks, and the policeman, Ibrahim Mahmud, was congratulating himself that no harm had come to any of us, and the boy, Musa Attiyeh, was turning cartwheels to show that he was not in the least exhausted and was much stronger than the policeman or the foreigner who rode on horseback.

Suddenly Ali Auda came running toward me, triumphantly holding up a rabbit, the only thing he had been able to shoot.

"It is for you, for you," he said, smiling from ear to ear, and threw it across my saddle.

It was a beautiful cottontail with silky yellow fur, almost golden. Ali Auda proved he was a good shot by shooting half its head away, and all the way back to Petra the blood dripped over the saddlecloth and the stallion's white belly.

WADI RUMM AND THE DIVINE
PRESENCES

In Jordan the best time for traveling is the early morning, and preferably all traveling should take place just before or just after sunrise. But that morning we were late in setting out for Wadi Rumm, chiefly because Abdul Razak had attended a wedding in the village of Elji. It was the wedding of one of his cousins, he had been up all night, he looked so pale and exhausted and his eyes were so red that he could have been taken for the bridegroom. There were festivities all night, there was so much food, so much drum beating, dancing, singing and ogling of the bride that he had been wide awake until cockcrow when he fell into a deep sleep. About two hours later someone, bawling in his ear, reminded him that he had promised to take me to Wadi Rumm, and he had woken with a start, washed, dressed, tested the tires of the borrowed Land-Rover, and finally reached the strange hotel in the Nabataean tomb.

"Was the bride pretty?" I asked.

"Very pretty—what you could see of her," he said. "She was veiled, of course. She was covered with jewels. I saw her eyes—enormous! I think my cousin is very lucky to have such a bride. I would have invited you, but you would have been a nuisance because I would have had to explain everything to you. You heard the shooting? That was me. I rode round the house firing joy-shots!"

"You enjoyed that?"

"Yes, of course. We always fire joy-shots when we are happy. How is your leg?"

"I won't be able to walk much."

"That's all right. I heard that Ali Auda carried you yesterday. He says you were very heavy."

He smiled from ear to ear, and said happily that the Land-Rover could drive us up to the police post at Wadi Rumm and there would therefore be no need for him to carry me on his back. He was sorry we were starting so late because the heat would be merciless and we would be half dead before we reached the police post. "Of course," he added sensibly, "we can always go tomorrow."

"No, we go today. Isn't there an Arabic proverb that says today is better than tomorrow?"

"Yes, there is, but it applies only to Arabs," he laughed, and soon we were driving past Ain Musa, the Fountain of Moses, where the rock was struck and the water spilled out to quench the thirst of the parched Israelites. Abdul Razak, who had theories about everything, was not completely convinced that Moses had struck the rock; he had bored into it with a pneumatic drill, or else (and this was much more likely) he had simply found an existing spring. There was a pleasant village at Ain Musa and the women were crowding round the spring, carrying enormous copper jars on their veiled heads. Here everything was a bright stabbing green, but there would be little enough greenness for the rest of the hot, dusty journey to the south.

To amuse himself, Abdul Razak decided to teach me some Arabic, beginning with the numbers one to ten. *Wahad, ithnain, thalatha, arba'a, khamsah, sittah, saba'a, thamanyah, tisa'ah, asharah.* These words gave dignity to numbers, unlike our rather crude one, two, three, four. I liked especially *thalatha* and *thamanyah,* which could be taken for the names of girls, and *asharah* had a good, round, heavy quality suitable for a number as large as ten. I wondered by what paths we had succeeded in giving bleakness to our English numerals, mysteriously concocting eight out of *octo* and four out of *quattuor,* reducing them to an insignificance they did not deserve. The Arabs, Abdul Razak reminded me, invented the numbers we use and gave them good names, and he had nothing but contempt for Roman numerals. Enough about numbers! He was pointing out, with many examples, that foreigners generally mispronounced Arabic because they lacked some essentials muscles in the back of the throat, and we were still arguing when he brought the Land-Rover to a sudden halt

Petra. El Khaznah, the Treasury, at the end of the Syk

Azraq. The Roman fort where T.E. Lawrence had his headquarters during the latter part of his campaign

The police post at Wadi Rumm

Jerusalem on the mosaic map at Madaba

The Apollo of Amman

Qasr al Amra, one of the desert castles

Columns of the Temple of Artemis at Jerash

The Tree of Cruelty at Caliph Hisham's Palace near Jericho

and said: "Ras al Naqab!" There, suddenly, thousands of feet below, lay a Chinese landscape.

The view from Ras al Naqab is one of the wonders of the world. Imagine you are standing on a high cliff and looking down on a calm sea with a few huge strangely shaped waves, some like seashells, some like towers, some like scoops of ice cream, and all of them admirably balancing one another, like the weatherworn rocks in a Chinese garden. The wild mountains stretch into the distance, rising sheer from the painted desert. There is something childish and innocent about them. They belonged there, were appropriate to this place, beneath that immense cliff, shimmering in the air stained golden by the sands of Arabia, for this at last was the Hasma, the fierce glittering desert that stretches far away to the south, to Yemen and the Indian Ocean.

There are only a few places on the earth where the mountains erupt in such a way they seem to be dancing. In Kweilin in China there are slender volcanic mountains towering over rice fields. These mountains have the appearance of being sculpted and then delicately painted; they are mirrored in the rice fields; and when you come upon them by road they are no more believable than when you are flying toward them in an airplane. You have the feeling that they cannot possibly be real and that nature even in her most prodigal moments could not have invented them. So it was at Ras al Naqab. This was a dream and in a moment the dream would dissolve into the same burned out land we had been traveling through since we left Wadi Musa.

We drove along the road, and the dream vanished, for that particular view of the distant mountains could not be sustained. A few moments after we left the cliff there was no sign of the valley below, for the mountains had vanished behind some rocky outcrops. Once more there were burned fields, the sense of desolation, the land so arid one wondered how anyone could live in it. An hour later we reached Guweira, a bus stop on the road to Aqaba, where the drivers pause briefly to drink mint tea and wash the dust from their faces. In Lawrence's time it was a cattle market used by the Howeitat Bedouin, and even then it was no more than a huddle of whitewashed huts. Now there were Coca-Cola stands and a few shops, a police station, a small mosque, but it still suggested a town that had not really come into existence and might be blown away with the next gust of wind.

For some reason Abdul Razak decided that Guweira was a fit place to stay for a meal. The eating shops were primitive, the flies were everywhere, and I thought it was the better part of wisdom not to eat anything that had already been digested by the flies. He simply waved the flies away and watched them settle down again. He said: "Guweira is famous for its flies," and left it at that. Soon there was a small dust storm, and the air was full of flies and dust, and everything turned black and grey.

I was glad when we left for Wadi Rumm, which lay beyond the trucks, the gasoline fumes and the misery of Guweira, which was as ugly as its name. It was the purest pleasure to drive out of the small town into the desert, which was not sand but rough stones. Abdul Razak drove with his hands off the wheel, for there was no road, and if a particularly large boulder came in sight, he would flick the wheel a little. But the bumping was bad for my sprained leg, and when at last he became aware of it, he drew the Land-Rover to a halt and settled down to a long discussion on the best way to lessen the pain. "We don't care about death," he said, "but pain—that's something we understand and care for. Let's think of the best way to avoid jolting your leg." He attacked the problem from many sides, finally coming to the conclusion that some old discarded mail bags in the back of the Land-Rover could be so arranged that the leg would lie securely on them. He had no sooner thought out the problem than he solved it. The leg, riding high on a bed of mail bags, received no more jolting.

There were shapeless mountains leading into the Wadi Rumm, but there was no glory in them, nothing to suggest the magnificence to come. I tried to get him to talk about the Arab attitude toward death and pain, but he said only that it was very simple: death was an enemy, pain a friend. You could do nothing against death, but everything must be done against pain. That was why through the ages the Arabs had reverenced their doctors and built hospitals and studied medicine. And then he stopped and said: "Death is not friendly," smiling a little, as though the idea had just that moment occurred to him. "Is that good English?"

"Yes, perfectly good English."

"Very well, I have made a good English sentence," he laughed, and pressed hard on the accelerator with the result that we were jolting again and even the mail bags could not take the shock of the boulders. But later we swung out into the valley, into the mud flats, and it was smoother riding. He could drive with his hands off the wheel, and this gave him great pleasure.

So we drove for about ten miles, coming closer to the mountains whenever he saw anything that attracted his attention, and usually it was something—a bird, or an inscription on the rocks, or a huddle of stones —which I could not see until we were right on top of it. Like Ali Auda he could see for miles with an enviable clarity. Heaps of stones and stone fenceworks clustered at the foot of the mountains, sometimes with queer Thamudic inscriptions. Some, no doubt, were ancient graves, and others perhaps were places where a long forgotten people had set up their tents and built a heap of stones to mark their progress when they moved on, and still others were perhaps no more than casual *graffiti* carved as a means of whiling away the endless time of the desert. The inscriptions were tantalizing, for they spoke of a people about whom almost nothing is known.

And then quite suddenly those rough unsculptured hills gave way to the austere majesty of Wadi Rumm. The earth changed color, became deeply crimson with here and there a few white boulders and stretches of greyish sand, and the whole valley opened out with the mountains on either side rising in yellow and crimson and gold. What was most remarkable about the mountains was not their sudden height, for they were at least two thousand feet high, but their proportions, the sculpturing of them, the way the rock faces were carved like the facades of Gothic cathedrals with an intricate tracing of shadowy forms, so that it was not difficult to see men and gods thousands of feet high written on the glowing rock. If you half-closed your eyes you saw the mountains carved in giant relief with battles and processions of horsemen. Something of the same effect can be observed in the gaunt face of the Theban cliffs behind the funeral palace of Queen Hatshepsut. The mountains themselves become sculpture.

There was no feeling of being dwarfed by the mountains, which were so vast they were beyond vastness, and the valley was broad enough to enable them to be seen in perspective. At intervals hot, red buttresses emerged to break their flow. For three hundred feet the base was granite; thereafter the mountains were sandstone. The effect was subtly to emphasize the majesty of the mountains by placing them on a granite pedestal like a throne. The striations were vertical, thus giving them thrust and movement. The air was sweet and pure in the cool winds of the valley.

We were racing across yellow sand at last and my leg was no longer throbbing. Abdul Razak had settled down to his old game of driving with his hands off the wheel, turning from side to side to beam at the mountains, very pleased with himself because he would soon be sitting in the shade over a cup of hot coffee. Far away, like a small insect cowering beneath the cliffs, was the headquarters of the Desert Patrol.

"What do you think about our valley?" Abdul Razak was saying with his hands cupped behind his neck to show how little he cared about maneuvering the Land-Rover.

"It's all right," I said.

"Is that all you think about it? All right? What does all right mean? Some adjectives, please. Stuperendous?"

I said there wasn't such a word but someone should invent it.

"What is wrong with it?"

"It doesn't exist—neither do the mountains. You are not sitting in a Land-Rover and I am not sitting beside you."

"Then you are out of your mind!"

"Yes," I said, and wondered whether anything in the world could be so wonderful as traveling along this broad avenue between mountains that changed color, threw beams of light at one another, and were delicately and wonderfully sculptured by those long vanished Gothic craftsmen. Red and purple birds darted out from under the wheels, and black goats were gamboling in the shade. Here and there near the foot of the mountains could be seen pools of intense green where a spring bubbled to the surface.

The local headquarters of the Desert Patrol was a small stone fortress with two watchtowers. There were four or five guards wearing red head-cloths, red sashes and tassels over their khaki uniforms, lean men, deeply sunburned, with dark intense eyes, and they were armed to the teeth like Circassians. The Desert Patrol has been granted the most colorful dress, but the men looked bored, they had very little to do, and they were glad to have Abdul Razak's company. Soon came small cups, each about the size of a large thimble, filled with the bitter Arab coffee which had been brewing in the courtyard on a fire of tamarisk twigs and camel dung.

"How is business?" Abdul Razak asked, and they answered quietly: "There is no business."

Some of the guards were sleeping in the shade just inside the fortress.

A dog prowled, its long tail close to the ground. Abdul Razak was telling them the latest news from Amman and Petra, not forgetting to describe the wedding of his cousin at Elji. The Arabs are great stirrers of coffee cups, and when they weary of coffee they are great stirrers of mint-flavored Ceylon tea. It became clear that the fortress at Wadi Rumm was really a police station. I asked them when they made their last arrest, and they answered that it was six months ago when they found a Bedouin stealing gasoline in Guweira. And then because they were engrossed in conversation about weddings, I asked if I could climb up the tower and gaze at the valley. They were well aware of the beauty of their valley; they placed a wooden ladder against the wall, and watched with some amusement while I accomplished the difficult job of mounting a ladder with only one leg operating efficiently.

It was wonderful to be alone in the immensity of the valley, in the silence of the desert. Far, far away on the desert floor there was a small splash of darkness that might have been a black tent belonging to the Howeitat tribesmen who have lived here as long as men can remember, but it might have been a depression in the sand, or a rock, or an ant, or anything at all. Size and scale vanished. The stupendous fiery cliffs, separated by acres of golden sand, seemed to be in mysterious motion, wheeling in unison, shimmering in the heat-haze; and sometimes there would come along the valley, like a dancer, one of those inexplicable devil-twists of sand, which rose, spouted, erupted and vanished in an instant. And always, at every moment, the mountains changed color from gold to hammered bronze and red and crocus yellow, as though they were made of gauze and millions of lamps were playing inside them.

But it was not the colors of the mountains so much as their shapes which were pleasing. It was not only that they had the nobility of the cliffs above Queen Hatshepsut's palace, but there was so much more of them and they seemed to go on forever, the world was enclosed by them, they were a prison and their very grandeur was a liberation. They reduced all things to the height of their majesty.

Lawrence of Arabia loved this valley almost to distraction and wrote about it often in *Seven Pillars of Wisdom,* for he was continually returning to it. He described it as "this processional way greater than imagination," and went on: "The Arab armies would have been lost in the length and breadth of it, and within the walls a squadron of aeroplanes could have wheeled in formation. Our little caravan grew self-conscious, and fell dead quiet, afraid and ashamed to flaunt its smallness in the presence of the stupendous hills." He especially enjoyed riding into the valley at sunset when the crags glowed with the colors of the dying sun.

"Rumm stumped you," E. M. Forster wrote to him good-humoredly, and so it did, as it would stump anybody. Lawrence wrote about the valley with intense feeling, as though it were his natural home, as though he had known it for everlasting. It was characteristic of him that he should have been the first to describe it at any length and to have thought himself blessed for having found it, reveling in this broad avenue where, it seems, the gods in their golden raiment stroll through the long afternoons of eternity.

It had been cool driving up the Wadi Rumm for the Land-Rover traveled at great speed, but from long sitting on the roof of the pink sandstone tower I felt the heat hammering me almost senseless. I could hear scraps of conversation coming from below. The dog was barking. On the other side of the valley three camels, the size of insects, were moving so slowly that I wondered whether they were moving at all, and indeed it was only possible to recognize they were camels because they moved in an odd, undulating way and carried the red saddlecloths of the Desert Patrol.

The heat performs strange tricks; it can send you to sleep and then burn you up; it can drive you half-mad and make you see visions. This time the vision took the form of a corporal of the Desert Patrol, wearing his *keffiyah* at a rakish angle, two broad straps of crimson leather crossing his chest, a silver dagger inserted in his crimson belt, holding in one hand a small blue-enameled coffee-pot and in the other hand a cup. He was rising in front of me like Beelzebub rising through a trap-door. He seemed to be floating upward and had no visible support. In fact he was walking up the ladder with the greatest of ease, smiling from ear to ear because he was well aware that he had given the impression of floating upward like an apparition. Then he hopped onto the tower and poured out the bitter coffee.

We left later in the afternoon for the long drive back to Petra, taking the young corporal with us. We talked about Lawrence of Arabia, who was still remembered. He had become a legend, but there were still a few men alive who claimed to have fought with him in the 1914–1918 war.

"My grandfather fought with him," the corporal said. "He died twenty years ago. There are not many left. Once I asked my father whether my grandfather had any clear recollection of Lawrence, and my father said: 'Yes, he had one recollection above all others. It was that Lawrence was always smiling even when he was in great pain.' "

One of the most memorable passages of *Seven Pillars* describes a small spring in the Wadi Rumm, where Lawrence once bathed his war-weary body and saw a wanderer of the desert as strange as himself:

> From this rock a silver runlet issued into the sunlight. I looked in to see the spout, a little thinner than my wrist, jetting out firmly from a fissure in the roof, and falling with that clean sound into a shallow, frothing pool, behind the step which served as entrance. The walls and roof of the crevice dripped with moisture. Thick ferns and grasses of the finest green made it a paradise just five feet square.
>
> Upon this water-cleansed and fragrant ledge I undressed my soiled body, and stepped into the little basin, to taste at last a freshness of moving air and water against my tired skin. It was deliciously cool. I lay there quietly, letting the clear, dark red water run over me in a ribbly stream, and rub the travel-dirt away. While I was so happy, a grey-bearded, ragged man, with a hewn face of great power and weariness, came slowly along the path till opposite the spring; and there he let himself down with a sigh upon my clothes spread out over a rock beside the path, for the sun-heat to chase out their thronging vermin.
>
> He heard me and leaned forward, peering with rheumy eyes at this white thing splashing in the hollow beyond the veil of sun-mist. After a long stare he seemed content, and closed his eyes, groaning, "The love is from God; and of God; and towards God."

We were talking about Lawrence when the corporal pointed to some tangled creepers and vines flashing green on a ledge about thirty feet up the mountainside just behind one of those red buttresses which jut improbably into the valley. He said this was a spring where Lawrence had bathed, and we scrambled up to see it, a difficult journey because my sprained leg was still tender. The paradise five feet square was now fifteen feet square, spreading in all directions, but the trough was still bubbling with water overflowing the ledge where he had left his clothes. The trough was about three feet long, scarcely more than a rounded slit in the rock. Lawrence had painted the scene with deliberate accuracy, but what he was painting was not so much the place where he bathed as the flow of sunlit air and color around it. It was cool in this shadowy half-cave sheltered by the crags, with the thick ferns and creepers smelling so sharply that the head reeled from being so accustomed to the odorless air of the valley.

When we had scrambled down and traveled a little way, I had my last look at the valley of Rumm, which is only twelve miles long but looks as though it must go on forever. It was fading now, the mountains no longer looked like the abodes of gods, and in fact they looked like mountains anywhere. Some days later, reading the *Koran*, I came upon the phrase: "Rumm of the Pillars, which has no equal." It appears that learned Arabs are somewhat mystified by this place, which is not otherwise mentioned in the *Koran*. Yet it is certain that the Prophet Muhammad was in his early years a trader who constantly traveled between Mecca and Damascus and could very easily have led his caravans through this valley. When he composed the *Koran*, he may have remembered the fiery rocks, the pillar-like buttresses, and all the royal magnificence of the valley, that no one can ever forget. "Rumm of the Pillars, which has no equal."

There were two places on the face of the earth which Lawrence thought especially blessed: one was the valley of Rumm, the other was Azraq of the Pools, which lies in the desert some sixty miles east of Amman. Of these places he wrote: *"Numen inest,"* "Divine majesty is in them." Of Rumm he said it was as vast as childhood dreams, and of Azraq that it was a place of absolute peacefulness. It was as though in some mysterious way they served as the habitation of divine presences; they magnified the spirit of man; holiness was in them. Coming to them, he felt he was at the still center of the turning world.

EAST OF THE DEAD SEA

The time came to return to Amman, and Abdul Razak was disappointed. He drove me about during the day or accompanied me inside the bowl of Petra, and then slipped off to his relatives at night. In Petra the air was clean and pure, the people were quiet and undemanding, and in Amman there was ferocious traffic, petrol fumes, noise and some other things he did not entirely approve of. Once he said: "Bribery and chickenry is all there is in Amman," and it was some time before I realized that chickenry was his sensible improvement on chicanery.

"Apart from bribery and chickenry, what's wrong with Amman?" I asked him.

"Oh, you'll learn someday. You've only spent a few days in Amman. Officers—lots of officers! Bureaucrats—lots of bureaucrats! They all think they are God's anointed! All right, I accept the anointment. I salute, I obey, I do what I am told, I kiss their hands, and all the time, inside me, I stand at ease. I come from the Bedouin. We are the real Arabs. No real Arab obeys orders. No real Arab lives in a city!"

He was cursing the cities and telling stories about them all the way back to Amman. He had been to Beyrout, which he regarded as the city of the damned *par excellence.* Perhaps New York and Paris were worse; he could not tell, not having been to either of them; he drove at seventy miles an hour along the Desert Highway in a well-tooled automobile which he loved to distraction and cursed all modern civilization.

It was one of those wonderfully clear days when the sky is very high and the royal blue is made more brilliant by the golden dust of the desert. There was almost no traffic on the road. This disturbed me, for it seemed to show that Jordan was economically much poorer than I believed it to be. Meanwhile it was good to travel along this road that cut like a knife through the desert and to listen to Abdul Razak roaring about the civilization he hated, despised and loved.

At Qantarah we turned west to reach Karak, the Crusader castle which once dominated all this region. It was a bumpy, twisting road, and he was reduced to driving at what he called "a thirty mile an hour crawl." Karak was magnificent, the ruined castle perched high on the cliff, dark against the western sky. He jammed his foot on the accelerator and we drove up the winding path to the cliff-top as though we were spinning up in the air.

The Crusaders called it Karak des Moabites or Le Pierre du Désert, and regarded it as their strongest fortress in Oultre Jourdain. It was built by Payen le Bouteiller in A.D. 1136 with no attempt to make it aesthetically pleasing—abrupt walls, slits, subterranean galleries, a massive keep, a drawbridge over the moat. The fortress was large enough to contain everyone in the walled village it protected, and as ugly as the muzzle of a gun. In its ruined state, with half the walls crumbling, it was still menacing. Inside it was dark, full of rubble, unornamented, with walls of rough-hewn stone which suggest that it was built hurriedly. From one of the towers fire signals sent messages to Jerusalem far away, and it had its own port on the Dead Sea.

We tramped about in the rubble, looking for some sign that would distinguish this fortress from a ruined prison, but there was none. Once, no doubt, there was a church, a banqueting chamber, an armory, a loggia where the captain-general received his guests and sat in state to receive tribute from the surrounding villages, but it was impossible to make out the purpose of the rooms we passed through, or rather their purpose was only too evident. Karak was a hammer poised on a cliff, dominating everything around.

On November 20, 1183, Saladin arrived unexpectedly outside the walls. It happened that this was the day when the eleven-year-old Princess Isabelle of Jerusalem was being married to the young and impossibly handsome Humphrey, Lord of Toron, heir-apparent through his mother of Oultre Jourdain. His mother, Stephanie de Milly, Lady of Karak, was now the wife of Reynaud de Châtillon, an accomplished soldier, brigand, and adventurer, who by his violence and lack of judgment was later to bring disaster to the Crusaders' forces. But now Reynaud exulted in the knowledge that Saladin was outside the walls. He ordered the wedding ceremonies to continue, sent a message to Baldwin IV, the King of Jerusalem, who was the stepbrother of Princess Isabelle, for reinforcements, and put the castle in a state of defense. From all over the realm of the Crusaders people had come to attend the wedding and to offer gifts to the bridal couple, and the chronicler relates that there were large numbers of musicians, minstrels, and jugglers to entertain the guests. The Lady Stephanie sent bread, wine, beef, and mutton to Saladin, saying she could do no less, for had she not, when he was a slave, cradled him in her arms in this very castle? It was a way of showing that the castle was well provisioned and lacked for nothing. Saladin with equal courtesy asked in which tower the young couple were housed, so that he could give orders to the commanders of his siege-engines not to bombard that part of the castle. The sounds of music from the castle were punctuated by the roar of the nine great mangonels hurling half-ton rocks at the castle walls, which were twenty feet thick. The siege lasted for two weeks, and the hammering continued relentlessly.

Baldwin IV, the bravest and most gallant of the Crusader Kings, was dying of leprosy in Jerusalem. He was twenty-two years old, and his face was already disfigured. He ordered the royal army to march on Karak and accompanied it on a litter, and when Saladin saw the army approaching he raised the siege and withdrew to Damascus. Within two years Baldwin IV was dead and within four years the Crusader army was destroyed on the Horns of Hattim.

Today a small village lies enclosed within the Crusader walls; there is a green mosque with a yellow minaret; and nothing happens there. The castle sleeps, and every day one more stone falls from the crumbling walls. We were told that in Crusader times prisoners were thrown off the parapet into the valley with their heads fitted into wooden boxes so that they would remain conscious as their broken bodies bounced from rock to rock, and in World War I the Turks used the underground galleries for torture chambers, torturing captured Arabs who were loyal to Feisal and Lawrence. We came at midday, when the people were wandering drowsily in the shade. There was only the passing moment to be endured;

they lived as plants live in the time between two cups of water. The village chieftain, a tall man in a gold-trimmed brown gown and a fiercely curling mustache, greeted us, made a little speech, composed himself, and fell asleep again.

We drove north along the fine, metaled road, and I was looking at the map and thinking about how soon we would reach Madaba when Abdul Razak pulled the car to a sudden halt. I looked down. The earth had split wide open, we were on the edge of a precipice with a thousand-foot drop to the bottom, the further bank was a mile away, and there was no possible explanation of why the earth had so abruptly taken leave of its senses. I looked at the map, which showed a faint wandering line and the words: Wadi el Mujib. I had thought a wadi would behave reasonably. What were we expected to do? Take a running leap across that incredibly deep gorge? Abdul Razak spent four or five minutes gazing down at the gorge with an expression of pure beneficence, and then he said: "Here we go!" We went, and it was terrible.

I counted eighteen hairpin bends carved into the side of the gorge and he took half of them on two wheels. I was grateful that he did not take his hands off the wheel. At the bottom a stone bridge arched over a dry river-bed, and then we climbed up almost as quickly as we made the descent. Soon we came to Madaba, a small town on a *tell* or mound which concealed perhaps ten other towns buried beneath it. It is mentioned in *Numbers* in the description of the overrunning of the land of Moab, laid waste "even unto Nophah, which reacheth unto Madaba," thus showing that Madaba was the furthest limit of their conquest.

Madaba now is a rather small, ungainly village with very little to recommend it except its prize possession: the earliest known map of the Holy Land. It can be accurately dated to about A.D. 560 in the time of Justinian, and it lies on the floor in brilliant mosaic in the Greek Orthodox Church of St. George. You ring a bell; an old man emerges from a house opposite the church; and soon you find yourself gazing down on a map which is some thirty feet wide and ten feet long. Time has eaten much of it away: only about a quarter of it remains. The map is provincial work with no claims to artistry, and yet it is vividly alive. Yellow boats sail on a boisterous Dead Sea where the waves twine like serpents, and on the blue-grey rivers the fish, as fat as balloons, swim merrily. Palm trees grow over Jericho, a lion is in hot pursuit of a gazelle near Bethabara, small clumps of foliage represent forests; and it is all done in many shades of red, blue, violet, green, brown, white, yellow and black. Karak is there, with a pre-Crusader Byzantine fortress on the edge of the steep cliffs. Best of all there is Jerusalem with its red roofs, its six gates, its main street running from one end of the city to the other with colonnades on both sides to shelter the traveler from the sun. The Church of the Holy Sepulchre, represented upside down, shows the facade of the basilica, the covered court of Calvary, and the gold dome above Christ's tomb, before the Crusaders changed the entire construction.

The Madaba map is wonderfully convincing; this is how the Byzantines saw the land during the few years in which it belonged to them. The mountains are depicted in a way that would have pleased Cézanne, with sudden planes of purple, blue, ochre, red, and yellow, and the yellow sand glitters appropriately. The map stretches down to Egypt, and we see Gaza with its magnificent basilica, its churches and colonnaded highway, of which nothing at all remains.

Madaba was sleeping its long sleep while we drove northward to Mount Nebo, where the high cliffs look down on the Dead Sea shimmering some 3,500 feet below. We could see the towers of Jerusalem far away, and Jericho among the palm trees. From this height the Dead Sea was a sulphurous blue trembling like shot silk; a small steamship was moving across the ghostly waters and leaving no wake; and it was very quiet on the heights where Moses, dying, looked out on the Promised Land:

> And the Lord spake unto Moses that selfsame day, saying, "Get thee up into this mountain Abarim, unto Mount Nebo, which is in the land of Moab, that is over against Jericho; and behold the land of Canaan, which I give unto the children of Israel for a possession: And die in the mount which thou goest up, and be gathered unto thy people; as Aaron thy brother died in Mount Hor, and was gathered unto his people. . . . Yet thou shalt see the land before thee; but thou shalt not go thither unto the land which I give to the children of Israel.

He was buried nearby, "but no man knoweth of his sepulchre unto this day."

It must be one of the loveliest views in the world, and cannot have changed much in all those three thousand and more years. Yet it was strangely unreal, for the Dead Sea far below seemed to be painted on oily canvas and the sky reflected its sombre colors, quivered and was never still. The Franciscans, who have excavated a Byzantine church nearby, have erected a cross on the highest point of the mountain and outlined the cross in electric lights, and this only added to the air of unreality.

We stayed for a long time on that cliff edge looking down at that preposterous sea, which was so very old, so wrinkled, so remote, so gaudy, and so strange. The little toy steamship was moving at a snail's pace. Smoke rose from a potash factory on the further shore. Suddenly there was a huge gust of wind and half the sea turned silver.

The light was fading when we drove back to Amman: the steep winding roads, the neon lights, the television aerials, the feeling that this was San Francisco but unaccountably all the neon signs were in Arabic. At break-neck speed Abdul Razak drove to my hotel.

"Tomorrow we go to Jerash," he announced.

"Why Jerash, and why tomorrow?"

"Because I have a girl friend there. If you can think of a better reason, let me know!"

ANTIOCH OF THE GOLDEN RIVER

The young Italian actress was wearing a soft white transparent dress as she leaned against one of the columns of the temple of Artemis. Her dark hair was piled high and bound with chains of pearls, while golden fillets across her chest had the effect of pushing up her breasts. Sometimes, leaning lasciviously against the column, she lifted up her face and smiled invitingly at the Arab boys, who gazed at her in sullen, resentful silence. If it had not been for the policeman with his hand on the holster of his revolver they would perhaps have hurled themselves upon her and torn her apart.

It appeared that a film company was making a movie amid the ruins of Jerash, the ancient Antioch Chrysorrhoas, Antioch of the Golden River, which lies two hours drive north of Amman along the road to Damascus. I have forgotten, if I ever knew, the name of the film, or what it was about. Other actors were milling about, their faces improbably painted bright yellow, and there was a small army of royal guards on horseback with spiked helmets and scarlet cloaks. I heard there were production problems, delays, the director had gone into a tantrum. Meanwhile among those immense columns, in that ancient Roman city which has survived more nearly intact than any other Roman city because the sands of the desert covered it, the only too nubile Italian girl held everyone in thrall.

And somehow it seemed perfectly appropriate that the girl should have conquered the city. Jerash-Antioch, built by one of Alexander's successors, was an eminently theatrical place. Temple crowded on temple, a vast colonnaded street ran through the entire city, and there were no less than three amphitheatres, one reserved for tragedy and comedy, the two others for more brutal entertainments by gladiators and by wild beasts. Amman has one amphitheatre, Petra has one, but Jerash-Antioch has three, thus testifying to its prodigious love of entertainment.

The city appears to have owed its wealth to the iron mines near Ajlun in the north and to being a great trading center on the road between Petra and Damascus. The proof of its former wealth lies in the size of its ancient marketplace where the citizens traded in ironware, gold, ivory, precious stones, pelts and ostrich feathers; their daggers were famous. I suspect it was also a place where people went for the pure pleasure of being there: the splendid river, the marble baths, the well-irrigated fields, the clumps of willows, walnut trees, and tall white poplars. The citizens were wealthy enough to transport granite columns from Assuan and marble columns from Asia Minor. They minted their own coins and sent out their own armies to attack the marauding Bedouin. The tall columns, silhouetted against the hills of Gilead, testify to their delight in their city. These golden columns are not so intimidating and overwhelming as the columns of Baalbek, but they have a wonderful lithe springing quality. There are probably more columns in Jerash than anywhere else on earth.

One day in the autumn or winter of A.D. 129 Jerash received its most distinguished visitor. The Emperor Hadrian arrived in great panoply, accompanied by a detachment of the imperial guard. He was forty-four years old, at the height of his power and prestige. He was perhaps the most intelligent of all emperors, for he was a gifted musician, an architect, a painter, a sculptor, a writer of verses and histories, as well as an astronomer and a designer of cities. He was on a tour of inspection of his empire and came accompanied by the remarkably handsome Antinous, his youthful lover, who had only another year to live. For some unknown reason Antinous drowned himself in the Nile, and the Emperor spent the last years of his life mourning for him.

But there was no mourning in Jerash. The citizens threw up a three-gated Arch of Triumph; there were games and celebrations; tragic actors paraded in the amphitheatre; on the deeply rutted streets the citizens watched the Emperor ride past in his chariot. He suffered from a serious skin infection and therefore spent a good deal of time in the bathhouses, for it was believed that the Golden River cured all sicknesses. There were also many important state matters to think about. The Emperor was planning to confer with all the kings and princes of the East in order to establish a permanent peace; nothing came of the conference, for Chosroes, the Parthian King, refused to attend. There was also the important matter of Jerusalem to be decided. Sixty years before, Jerusalem had been destroyed by Vespasian and Titus, and for all those years it remained derelict. Hadrian agreed that the time had come to rebuild it under the new name of Aelia, Aelius being his own family name. Here, or perhaps later in Alexandria where he settled for a few weeks, he was visited by the great Jewish mystic Akiba who urged him to permit the Jews to live in Jerusalem; he refused. They could live wherever they liked but not in Jerusalem; instead of the Temple of the Jews there would the Temple of the Romans; and so it was.

The days passed in conferences, parades, much coming and going of emissaries, while the ornamental fountains played and the nights were loud with rejoicing. Then Hadrian was gone, and the city lapsed into being one more distant outpost of the empire. For a few days it was the capital of the world, and then it became a city too close to the desert for comfort.

Nevertheless the work of building went on: the great complex of buildings which forms the Temple of Artemis was not built until twenty years later. When the Christians came, churches and a cathedral were built from the stones of the pagan temples, but the healing powers of the Golden River were not forgotten. Every year, on the anniversary of the miracle of Cana, the waters of the cathedral fountain miraculously turned into wine.

The Moslems came, and then there were earthquakes, and the sand drifted across the abandoned city. For centuries it was forgotten. In 1806 the German traveler Ulrich Seetzen stumbled upon it, but more than a century passed before it was properly excavated. To this day the Arabs will say of a ruined place: "It is like the ruins of Jerash."

We wandered up and around the city, which looked on that September morning as though it were only waiting for the red-tiled roofs to be replaced on the delicately carved Corinthian columns, thus forming shady colonnades. We wandered up along the Street of Columns, then around the foundation stones of Byzantine churches with the mosaics laid out on the floors—seventeen churches have been counted already and there are more to come—and then up the steps of the Temple of Jupiter, and then across a field to see why a solitary honey-colored column was standing amid the poplars. Black and white pigeons were flying, boys were bathing in the pools, and the air was scented and fresh from the abundant waters. At last we returned to the Temple of Artemis. The Italian actress was still leaning against the column and the Arab boys were still edging close to her, the unappeasable hunger still written on their faces. At last the small, squat, bearded director arrived, the cameras were brought up, the reflectors were properly placed, and the policeman with his hand on the holster of his revolver waved us all away.

THE DESERT CASTLES

Some sixty miles across the desert eastward from Amman lies Azraq of the Pools with its dark fortress erected by the Roman legionaries. Here Lawrence of Arabia spent some weeks in the rainy autumn of 1917, waiting for the big push to the north, receiving the tribal chieftains from the surrounding territory, reading poetry, and listening to the songs of the Arabs. The wind came through the black beams of the roof, a fire glowed, the slanting rain in the firelight somehow gave the place a magical appearance. Pools, palm trees, a fortress built of black basalt with a black-walled courtyard.

The Romans built it about A.D. 300. Later it fell to the Byzantines and then to the Kings of Ghassan, who were Christian Arabs owing allegiance to the Byzantine emperor and were well rewarded for keeping the peace in the desert in the days before Islam emerged to strike fear in the hearts of Byzantine emperors. The Kings of Ghassan encouraged poetry and music, and some of their court poetry full of chivalry and violence has survived. Azraq means "blue," and the place owes its name to the blue pools shaded by palms and tamarisks.

One day I set out with Abdul Razak for Azraq in a jeep. He said he was pleased to leave Amman, where he was being bitten to death by sand flies. It was a long journey, and he proposed to stop at the hunting lodges of the Umayyad Caliphs on the way. Not far from Amman at a police post he picked up an armed guard, Muhammad Maziad, a lean silent man with a ferocious black mustache and languorous heavily-lidded eyes, who spoke little during the journey and spent most of the time caressing his rifle. For ten minutes we sped along the desert highway, where the signs read: PETRA/ ROSE-RED/ NABATAEAN CITY, and stopped abruptly at an oasis where a great white-walled tank filled with blue water appeared out of nowhere in the immensity of the yellow desert. The water was the deepest and most luminous blue I have ever seen, and very tempting. Even now I measure the richest blues by that oasis off the desert highway, and sometimes a person's eyes or the deepest blue in a painting will send me back to that early morning when we set out for Azraq.

Perhaps it was the yellow of the sand which set off the blue water and gave it resonance, as the color of an emerald will be enhanced if it is set in a gold ring, or perhaps it was the shimmering sand flowing in the sky which gave it that depth upon depth of royal blue, for this white-walled lake fifty feet long and fifty feet broad seemed to contain the concentrated colors of the sky, to be the whole heavens in miniature, to embrace the essence of the heavenly light. There it was, remote and beautiful, isolated from any human habitation, and absolutely perfect. One did not think of it as water. One thought of it as a discovery of light as close to perfection as it is possible to be; and when I looked up, the sky was paler than the lake.

Some camels were coming across the desert, plunging when they caught sight of the lake. Soon there was a throng of camels noisily quenching their thirst, while the camelmen shouted and waved their arms as though they had gone mad, so excited they were at the prospect of drinking after a long ride. The camels were decorated with turquoise beads and the saddlecloths were all the colors of the rainbow.

But when we turned sharply into the desert, the colors vanished. Soon the sand gave way to the mud flats, hard as knives, with a few tufts of withered scrub, and here and there a few stones piled up to show that some traveler had passed this way before. Because the desert was flat, without dimension, these small pathetic cairns were to be looked for eagerly; without them the desert would be unendurable. These heaps of stones were companionable, reminding you that you were not entirely alone in this featureless immensity.

I asked Abdul Razak what he thought of the cairns and whether he steered by them.

"As for the steering," he said, "we steer by the senses which God has given us. I don't have my hands on the wheel. I set the direction and wait till we get there. As for the stones, no one knows who placed them there, or why. It may have been thousands of years ago. A man dies, and they place some stones over his grave, or he arranges the stones in a secret way for those who come after him, or else they are signposts. No one knows."

He shrugged his shoulders. The soldier, Muhammad Maziad, was crooning over his rifle. I had the feeling that there was no other object in the world he loved so much, and if we were in danger, he would protect it by throwing himself on the ground and covering it with his body.

About halfway to Qasr al Mashatta I observed for the first time the strange liquid glow on the horizon which would accompany us throughout most of the journey. Trembling, silvery blue, a thin slice of jellied water seemed to be hovering at the extremity of vision, and since it resembled nothing so much as an oasis, it was easy enough to imagine grasses and reeds and even palm trees. I had thought mirages occurred rarely or intermittently and that they hovered above the sky-line, but this blue mirage clung obstinately to the curving line where the sky met the burning earth. It was absurd, bewitching, tantalizing, could not be shaken off. Wherever you looked there was the illusion of cool waters. Equally inexplicable were the devil-twists, small clouds of spinning dust which rose like columns with fan-shaped heads and vanished, melting into the air, as mysteriously as they were formed. Sometimes they floated along the ground for four or five seconds, or for fifteen seconds, and it was easy enough to imagine they were the ghosts of dancing girls.

The jeep was ludicrously uncomfortable, for I was jammed between Abdul Razak and Muhammad Maziad, who held his wretched rifle in such a way that I was in continual danger of having my brains blown out. I asked him whether it was loaded. It was. Abdul Razak reminded me that a rifle was useless unless loaded, and I reminded Muhammad Maziad that his purpose was to protect my life from marauding tribesmen, not to kill me. Whereupon, with ill-temper, he rested the butt of the rifle on the floor of the jeep. With luck the first bullet would go harmlessly through the tarpaulin roof.

Abdul Razak knew surprisingly little about the desert castles. He came from Petra in the south and regarded the north as foreign territory. He had read somewhere that they were the hunting lodges of the Umayyad Caliphs. But who were the Umayyad Caliphs? It appeared that they had reigned from Damascus, loved pleasure, built superbly, and in time gave place to the far more formidable Abbasid Caliphs reigning from Baghdad. It appeared, too, that Damascus had spoiled the Caliphs rotten, so that instead of following the harsh and purposeful commands of the Prophet they gave themselves up to unimaginable license while proclaiming themselves the Prophet's inheritors. Nominally they ruled the world from Persia to Spain. Their power and wealth were dazzling; for ninety years they squandered their inheritance. Then they went down to defeat.

Low on the horizon, the ruins of one of their desert castles were racing toward us. They seemed to rise from an island in a lake.

Hunting lodge, palace or castle, Qasr al Mashatta was all these. Once it was a kind of fairy palace, so intricately and delicately carved that it was perhaps intended for the women of the Umayyad court. We climbed over green marble pillars and tumbled cornices carved like lace to reach a ruined hall shaped like a majestic trefoil. This was the center of the palace, throne room and meeting place for the huntsmen and huntswomen who rode out to hunt the lions, bears, ostriches and gazelles that once roamed the desert. The ruined palace looked as though it had been hit by a bomb. Smashed cornices lay in the thorn grass; soaring arches had crumbled, leaving only the marble pillars with acanthus capitals; one small, battered, broken room opened upon another; the only sound came from the faint squeaking of the speckled lizards as they slithered over the broken columns.

Decidedly one can develop a taste for desert palaces! To build a lacy palace of golden stone, to fill it with high-spirited young people, with Arab horses and hunting-dogs and musicians, and then in the evening to listen to the court poet recounting the events of the day—what fun! The Caliph Muawiya, most self-indulgent of Arab Caliphs, probably built it about A.D. 675, employing Greek, Coptic and Persian workmen to carve the capitals and decorate the facade in superb intricate designs like golden lace.

When a bomb falls or an egg shell is smashed, the original pieces can usually be found, though broken and scattered. What was puzzling about Qasr al Mashatta was that many of the original pieces had obviously been removed. Abdul Razak said he thought they must have been taken to the nearby village of Jiza where some especially decorative pieces adorned the police post—the fate reserved for all beautiful things. He did not know. It was a guess. I learned later that most of the facade had passed into the possession of the one man I would have thought least worthy of it and least responsive to it—Kaiser Wilhelm II. In 1903 Sultan Abdul Hamid II gave it to him and it was transported to Berlin. Forty-two years later about half of it perished during a bombing raid and what remains, the most elaborate and intricate tracery ever carved in stone, can still be seen in the State Museum in East Berlin.

There were two more fortress-palace-hunting-lodges on the way to Azraq. For mile upon mile we drove over the hard-baked biscuit-colored flats, accompanied by devil-twists, watched by the liquid horizon, the blue lake where no one ever slaked his thirst. Then the brilliant yellow walls of Qasr al Kharanah came in sight, more fortress than palace, four-square, with rounded buttresses at the corners, a few small arrow-slits cut into the walls that were three stories high. Unlike Qasr al Mashatta, it was in a fair state of preservation, and needed only a column of knights in chain-mail and pennons fluttering from the walls to come into its own. According to a Kufic inscription in an upper room it was built in A.D. 711 by the Caliph Walid I, whose armies conquered Spain and penetrated deep into India.

The custodian was an old gap-toothed man who wore a grey pullover against the coldness of the stone corridors and carried a revolver strapped to his side, not, he explained, for fear of visitors but for fear of marauders who would break into the fortress in search of loot. There was nothing to loot except a tabby cat. He smiled as he cradled the cat in his arms. I would have taken it for a very small cheetah. Its ears sprang up when it heard the kettle boiling; thimble cups of coffee were served; and there was a saucer of hot, oily coffee for the cheetah. According to the custodian, it had crossed the desert from God knows where one day during the previous winter, and now the old man was happy, saying: "This is no ordinary cat. We have long talks together." And when we walked through the simple arched rooms of the fortress, it followed at our heels.

The Caliph Walid had done his work well. The fortress had clear-cut noble lines, spacious rooms, delicate decorations carved in the iron-hard plaster. You might have taken it for a monastery, so quiet it was. One day in 1918 Lawrence of Arabia, riding north, saw it in the white ghostliness of moonlight and a few moments later was terrified to find the white earth carpeted with birds which wheeled up from under the camels' feet so that he seemed to be drowned in feathers; and for a while his men fired helplessly into the multitude of birds, feeling they had entered a strange magical country. On the afternoon of the next day they reached Qasr al Amra, which Lawrence described as the hunting lodge of Harith, the Shepherd King, a patron of poets, contemporary of the Ghassanid Kings who ruled before Islam conquered the land.

It took Lawrence on camelback more than twelve hours to make the journey from Qasr al Kharanah to Qasr al Amra, but he was marching cautiously to avoid the Turks who were nearby. In our fast-flying jeep it took less than half an hour. The mud flats came to an end; there was a patch of green; and then there arose from the earth a small palace of reddish stone with a solitary dome and three rounded vaults, looking very lonely in this barren landscape. The jeep roared to a halt outside the gateway. So very rounded a building looked very feminine, and we felt like intruders. Inside, in eight or nine places, the walls were painted with frescoes which were peeling away, leaving only a few fragmentary, high-spirited designs. In diamond-shaped lozenges an unknown artist painted horses, lions, cranes, gazelles, dancing girls, a fiddler, Suluki hunting dogs; three naked women cavorted near a window under a grape arbor; emperors in full regalia; birds flying; a man wrapped in a blue gown, sitting on a rock and gazing into the distance. The gazelles were the best, for they were full of movement; the women were too fat to be entertaining; the lions looked like kittens. The date of the paintings was about A.D. 715 in the reign of the resourceful Walid, but part of the building might very well have been erected in the time of the Ghassanids. And if it was strange to find so much painting in this hollow in the desert, it was stranger still to find a palace so feminine that it cried out for the presence of women. Probably there was water under the earth, for those clumps of fresh green grass nearby could not have existed without water. Yet the well was dry, the land arid, and you found yourself wondering how they could ever have filled the baths at the back of the building. Bathhouse, hunting lodge, picture gallery, all set in the midst of nowhere! Perhaps, like Fatehpur Sikri, it was abandoned as soon as it was built, one more lonely gift to the desert.

We raced on to Azraq of the Pools, the blue oasis, which Lawrence loved as he loved Rumm. The earth became vicious. Instead of the mudflats or the sunbaked flinty soil, as hard as rock, we entered a forbidding land of black lava, a whole landscape strewn with black cobblestones.

They shot up like bullets and rattled against the jeep, and there was no end to them. As far as the eye could see, there was only the hard black lava, drab, menacing, hideous, and absurd. Not a blade of grass, not a shrub, grew in that desolation. Abdul Razak grinned. He knew the way, although there was no road, no path, no signpost anywhere. He said: "We'll be there in ten minutes," while I wondered whether we would be there in ten hours, so vast was that landscape of interminable black coals. And all the time on the horizon there was the gleaming silvery blue lake mocking our parched throats.

At last the interminable litter of black lava gave way to the sunbaked mudflats, tufts of green appeared, the earth grew wholesome again. We swept up a rise and looked down on real lakes, real pools, real houses, real trees. The silvery blue mirage vanished in the shining waters.

In *Seven Pillars of Wisdom* Lawrence described his total joy on reaching Azraq:

> We hurried up the stony ridge in high excitement, talking of the wars and songs and passions of the early shepherd kings, with names like music, who had loved this place; and of the Roman legionaries who languished here as garrison in yet earlier times. Then the blue fort on its rock above the rustling palms, with the fresh meadows and shining springs of water, broke on our sight. Of Azraq, as of Rumm, one said *'Numen inest.'* Both were magically haunted; but whereas Rumm was vast and echoing and God-like, Azraq's unfathomable silence was steeped in knowledge of wandering poets, champions, lost kingdoms, all the crime and chivalry and dead magnificence of Hira and Ghassan. Each stone or blade of it was radiant with half-memory of the luminous silky Eden, which has passed so long ago.

Dominating Azraq was the old Roman fort, built of black lava stone, not tall nor very imposing, with a brooding heaviness which seemed strange in such a smiling landscape. Lawrence lived in a room above the southern gate tower, with saddlecloths stretched on the floor to give color to its blackness. An arched window opened on the inner courtyard littered with the same black stones, fragments of an ancient altar, a dedicatory inscription to the Emperors Diocletian and Maximian, and another to the Emperor Jovian. There was a fireplace, but no chimney, and indeed there was little need for a chimney, for you could see the sky between the black stone beams of the roof. At night there came strange moanings and howlings, and the Arabs pounded the coffee harder in an effort to drown out the ghostly cries of long-dead hunting dogs kept by the ancient rulers of the fortress. Lawrence never learned where these cries came from. Wolves, hyenas, jackals, or the wind in the trees? Through one of the slits in the wall I looked out over a green meadow where Guernsey cows were grazing.

Lawrence's black fort was bleak enough to send us back to the pools, the reeds and the tamarisks waving softly. Azraq was fat with water. A sign read:

STRICTLY FORBIDDEN
SWIMMING AND WASHING IN THIS POOL.

Nevertheless some boys were swimming in it, laughing and calling on us to join them. Instead we wandered off for a lunch of bully beef, cheese and Arab bread, and found ourselves in a pumping station. Azraq had entered the modern age: the gleaming machinery thundered and roared; a soft-spoken man in charge announced that 840,000 gallons of water were being pumped daily from Azraq to Irbid, to irrigate the east bank of the Jordan. It appeared that the pools were inexhaustible.

Circassians had settled in Azraq, fair-haired and blue-eyed, and there was a Druze village nearby. The Druzes were secretive, while the Circassians flashed easy smiles. A Circassian was in charge of what he called the museum, a pleasant room with some pieces of ancient pottery in a glass case, an iron bed, paper roses, a stove, and on the wall many pictures torn out of magazines. King Hussein gazed down benignly while we sat on cushions, drank tea, and discussed the affairs of the world.

"Tell me what is happening outside," the small blue-eyed Circassian said. "In this part of the world nothing happens—not even a murder."

He seemed to regret the absence of murderers, while the sunlight, beating through the fronds of the palm trees, lit up the chaste white-washed room where he displayed his treasures. We heard the murmur of water and the thumping of the pumping station far away. It was so peaceful in the room that we were in danger of spending the rest of the day drinking his sweet tea.

It was late when we set out across the desert for Amman, and Abdul Razak decided to make up for lost time by driving faster than ever. A yellow cloud, a mile high, rose behind the jeep, and then came a stretch of black lava and the cloud vanished. Once Abdul Razak murmured that on a previous journey he had shot a wolf and regretted he had no wolf pelt to take back to Petra. A few moments later Muhammad Maziad shouted that he had seen a wolf; the jeep came to a sudden halt; something grey and furtive was moving in the distance; he fired three shots at it, and then ran off into the desert, while I wondered whether I would be the one who would have to carry the dead and bleeding wolf across my knees. Another shot was fired, and then another. We thought the last was the coup de grace, but he returned empty-handed, more lugubrious than ever.

"Did you miss it?" Abdul Razak asked pleasantly.

Muhammad Maziad shrugged his shoulders.

"They are too clever for me," he said, and muttered a curse against all the wolves of the world.

We raced back to Amman against a sandstorm. We knew it was coming because the birds were flying low. We were racing across the desert straight at the dying sun, and suddenly the sun went out and there was only a world of spinning sand that grew darker and heavier. Abdul Razak drove hard through the storm. He could see nothing, but it did not matter. Storm or no storm, he drove at forty miles an hour. The tarpaulin flapped wildly, and our eyes smarted, while we drove into nothingness, into a huge yellowish-brown wall of sand mixed with small pebbles and sharp flints; and the sandstorm carried us along with it and then flung us aside and then covered us again. From time to time, very faintly, we could see the ochre glow of the sunset.

Five minutes later the storm had spent itself. The stars came out in the clear sky, Amman was twinkling with lights, and we raced up the steep roads at fifty miles an hour. Then we counted our blessings: we had seen the abandoned desert castles of the Umayyad Caliphs, seen or thought we had seen a wolf as large and beautiful as a snow leopard, been lifted off the earth in a raging sandstorm, breathed vast mouthfuls of pure desert air, and watched with fascination the hard blue liquid line of the horizon. It was a good day, and on the next day we went to Jericho.

THE DEAD SEA FRUIT

In the nineteenth century the very rich liked to spend their winters in Luxor, where there was the certainty of cloudless skies, no rain would ever fall, and the heat would be very nearly unbearable. Those who were not quite so rich discovered that they could spend warm winters in Jericho, where there were no ornate hotels with thousands of servants and the skies were equally cloudless. Jericho was not fashionable, but it was quiet and friendly. There were neat rows of small hotels among the palm trees. There was little to do except to take sun baths, for no one went boating on the Jordan River or sailing on the Dead Sea. The archaeologists were digging into the ancient city, but they were remarkably secretive. Jericho was a place where you would find elderly Englishwomen sitting in gardens under white parasols, sipping Ceylon tea.

In England "Go to Jericho" meant "Go clean out of this world." The phrase seems to have come into existence in the middle years of the nineteenth century, when the first winter residents settled there in the unabashed enjoyment of perpetual summer. It was a good place to visit if you had nothing to do. The same idea occurred to Caliph Hisham about A.D. 730, when he built a vast pleasure palace two miles north of the town. It was a wonderfully complicated palace with pools and fountains fed from the Jordan, court opening on court opening on court, all ornamented with mosaics and stucco statues of full-breasted, wide-eyed young women carved rather inexpertly. We know these young women because they now grace the Rockefeller Museum in Jerusalem. We know a good deal about

Caliph Hisham, who was one-eyed, vengeful, intelligent, mercenary, and bigoted. His reign was famous for its fine armor and the brilliant colors of its carpets. He inherited an empire that stretched from Spain to the borders of China, and he presided over its decay.

The Caliph's taste for luxury expressed itself in his winter palace in Jericho, which was discovered as late as 1937. It resembles Qasr al Amra magnified about fifty times. It had white domes and rounded vaults, and the walls were painted in brilliant colors, with ornamental gardens, stables, and luxurious bathhouses, with columns crowned with intricately carved acanthus leaves painted in red and yellow; the leaves are wind-blown, as delicate as lace, and soon will fall. And while the Caliph had a somewhat unruly taste for fat women, he had an exquisite taste for mosaics. Amid the ruins of his palace you suddenly come upon a marvelous mosaic that is at once extremely beautiful and oddly menacing. On one side of an enormous tree heavy with delicately shaded fruit two gazelles are grazing, while on the other side a solitary gazelle is being ripped open by a tawny lion, the gazelle leaping and the lion in mid-air. And there is about this sleek and most delicately formed mosaic a strange coldness like a drop of ice falling on the heart. It is menacing because it is so calm. The Caliph seems to be saying: "I am this luxurious tree, and in my shadow you may graze wherever you please. If you are destroyed, this is no concern of mine." Implicit in the design is a condemnation of all human life under the sun. Although not a single human figure appears on the mosaic, the Arabs call it "the Tree of Human Cruelty," and although some fifteen red apples hang from the branches, admirably placed and marvelously executed, they will tell you they are not apples at all—they are eyes.

The Arab historians have taken the measure of Caliph Hisham and found him wanting. It was in his reign that the Arabs descended on France, and they might have conquered all of Europe if Charles Martel had not thrown back an Arab army at Tours. They tell how Hisham's son fell from his horse and was killed while hunting, and when he heard of it he remarked coldly: "I raised him to be a Caliph, and he has to get himself killed for a fox." Only a few years after Hisham's death the dynasty perished, and the Abbasids in their rage against the defeated Umayyads ordered that the Caliph's body be dug up and publicly flogged. His successors were as merciless as he was. They loved pleasure just as much, and had the same thirst for killing, but none were so cold-blooded.

I wandered around the Caliph's palace in the early morning light, seeing only the broken marble columns, the low walls, and acres of mosaics laid out like gardens, and came back again and again to that fabulous mosaic which had been preserved complete without the slightest damage just as it left the artist's hands more than a thousand years ago. The other mosaics were not especially interesting, but "the Tree of Human Cruelty" was the single masterpiece of the Caliph who, after the emperor of China, was the most powerful man of his time. You had to climb up and perch on a balcony to see it well; each little fragment of colored stone accurately fitted to the next, the colors shading into one another, the whole possessing that completeness that comes only when an art is overripe. It was a miraculous thing, though menacing. The round red apples puzzled me until it occurred to me that they were Dead Sea fruit.

A few minutes later I walked down to the Dead Sea, splashing across the River Jordan which was only ankle-deep and very cool, trickling silver among the reeds. Then at last, wandering beside the poisonous sea, I was able to shake off the memory of a poisonous Caliph.

THE RIVER JORDAN

It seemed to me that I was always coming upon the River Jordan when I least expected to. This mysterious secretive river would suddenly appear out of a desert, and long before you set eyes on it you knew it was there by the sudden freshness of the air.

I remember the first time I saw the Jordan, quite suddenly, at a bend in the sandy road near Beisan. There were waving reeds, softly waving willows and feathery tamarisks, and there was a gap among the trees, and the desert was only three or four yards from the river. After the long hours of driving, the sudden greenness resembled a mirage and was quite unbelievable. So, too, was the swift whispering music of the river, a rustling sound of especial sweetness. I rushed down a sandy slope, threw off my shoes, rolled up my trousers, and waded into midstream, surprised by the coldness of the water and the sharp stones in the river bed.

At this place the Jordan was perhaps fifteen feet wide, and a man could therefore cross from one bank to the other with two breast strokes; but there was a fierce current and it seemed safer not to swim in it. In the shadow of the willows and tamarisks the river was a deep blue, which made the white foam brighter. Tangled roots came down the river, floating past at incredible speed, and here and there you could see whirlpools where roots and leaves went racing in circles before they dipped out of sight, to be carried forward by the deeper currents of the river. There was the feeling of freshness and youth, the world suddenly becoming desirable, after the ancient aridity of the desert.

The Russians have a word, *shelest,* for the rustling sound of rivers and leaves, but we have no good word for it. The *shelest* of the Jordan was a sound that can never be forgotten, so bright and airy, so merrily tumultuous, that it resembled the babbling of a happy child. Half the pleasure of wading in the cool waters was in listening to the river's voices. Afterward, climbing up the bank, ankle-deep in scorching sand, I realized that the sound of the river stopped within a few feet of it, and only the lingering freshness of the air served as a reminder that the river existed. My feet painfully burned by the sand, I jumped into the car and a few moments later the river had vanished.

There are rivers like the Nile and the Yangtse which have dominated history and brought into being entire civilizations. They dictate their own terms, demand their own massive tribute from the people who live on their banks, and behave always with a kind of imperturbable imperiousness, indifferent to men's lives and hopes. They are vast engines of creation and destruction, and they wear their greatness with effortless dignity. The Jordan is not one of these rivers. It is small and humble, never parading itself but on the contrary taking pleasure in concealment, and there are places where it is scarcely wider than a mountain brook in Scotland. It is a stream, not a river. Yet in its own way it has influenced the course of history and dictated its own terms to the warring tribes on its banks. It is a power to be reckoned with.

From the air the Jordan is no more than a thin silvery ribbon wandering snakelike through the desert. It twists and turns in graceful curves, meandering in such a way that although the distance between the Sea of Galilee and the Dead Sea is only sixty-seven miles as the crow flies, the actual course of the river is over two hundred miles. During this journey it drops six hundred feet, and thus comes to resemble a prolonged waterfall.

No one has ever sailed ships up the Jordan, no great cities have been built on its shores, and no great fortresses have guarded it. Its importance, such as it is, lies in its strategical position between the desert and the sown in a land of perpetual migrations, at the crossroads where empires meet. Innumerable battles were fought on its shores not because the river was worth having, but because it stood on the frontier of more fertile pastures, because it served as a road between the Sea of Galilee and the Dead Sea, and because so many legends had accumulated around it. If it had been twenty feet wider, the history of the Middle East would have been very different.

The Jordan is a very odd river indeed, possessing an enchantment of its own. Seen against the skull-shaped rocks of the Ghor, or the sandy wastes, the river appears as an impertinence or a mirage. It has none of the grandeur of the desert. To the thirsty traveler who dreams of the mighty floods which sometimes race down the giant wadis, the Jordan comes as an affront, its very smallness demanding an apology. And then gradually, as you rest in the shade of the willows, you realize how appropriate and beautiful it is. Nothing could challenge the desert except that gay and rippling stream. Here is rest and contentment on a small and human scale, and for a few hours you can forget the overwhelming presence of the desert, which devours all things. The desert is an eternal enemy; the stream is an abiding friend.

So it must have been during all the generations of wandering tribesmen who watered their camels at the fords and sometimes settled for a few months on its banks. We hear of Jacob's town of Succoth, and if you travel down the highway that follows the line of the East Ghor Canal, you come across what remains of Succoth, and it is no more than an egg-shaped mound beside the road, not much larger than a two-story house. It has been partially excavated, and you can see perhaps twenty small rooms, like a honeycomb. The rooms are the size of prison cells, and there cannot have been more than forty of them altogether. Dr. Kathleen Kenyon has shown recently that David's Jerusalem covered no more than ten acres. We think of great cities rising in Old Testament times, but in fact everything was in miniature. The tribes were small, the towns were merely fortified outposts, and there was room enough for everyone. In those days the Jordan, that miniature river, was perfectly in scale.

Not that the river lacks majesty: it can roar and rage when it wants to. When the winter floods come down, it pours down with a vengeance, overflowing its banks, and sometimes washing the bridges away. A man falling in the river might be dashed to pieces against the roots of the trees or sucked in a whirlpool. Then in March, after two months of rampage, the river settles once more between the narrow banks. The ancient Hebrews spoke with awe about "the swelling of the Jordan," and they wished it would not swell so rapidly. On the whole they had no very great liking for the river and compared it unfavorably with the more predictable rivers of Damascus, the Abana and the Pharpar.

When the Hebrews first encountered the Jordan, it was mid-winter and the river was in flood. The priests carrying the Ark doubted whether the people could make a safe crossing, "for Jordan overfloweth all his banks all the time of harvest." Joshua accordingly summoned the help of God, and a miracle took place, for the waters parted and the Israelites walked across as though on dry land, eventually to capture Jericho and to put fear in the hearts of the Amorites and the Canaanites. The place where the Israelites crossed over is said to be Bethabara, which is also the traditional site of the baptism of Christ.

Surprisingly the Jordan is rarely mentioned in the Old Testament. Naaman was cured of his leprosy after bathing seven times in the holy river, and Elijah smote the waters with his mantle, ordering them to part and to provide him with a safe passage. Otherwise there are few references to the river. In the New Testament it is mentioned just as rarely, though the prominence of the baptism colors the entire Gospel.

Today at Bethabara there is a nest of small churches and open-air altars to welcome the pilgrims of many denominations, and on any day some service will be taking place. The Arabs have their booths selling small bottles of Jordan water and postcards of the holy sites. The water has so many chemicals in it that it becomes opaque and acquires a dreadful smell two or three weeks later. Bethabara is almost a fun-fair. The booths are brightly colored, banners flutter, processions are continually going down to the water. One Arab, more enterprising than the rest, has pitched his tent on the river bank and spends his time surveying the pilgrims with a smile of the purest beneficence in the company of his camel and her foal. With accurate spelling and a rather odd way of breaking up the lines he has written on a large placard:

> IT WOULD BE KIND OF
> YOU AFTER TAKING
> THE PICTURE OF THE
> TENT AND THE CAMEL
> TO TIP THE OWNER

The Arab had a scruffy appearance and might have been taken for a beggar if it had not been that he quite obviously owned a fair-sized tent, a camel and a foal. He darted encouraging smiles at everyone with a camera and ignored the rest. His placard was an eternal reminder of the existence of Mammon. He looked very happy and jolly. He had seen the pilgrims come and go, and knew they were generous.

Perhaps it was inevitable; all holy sites become marketplaces. The postcards, the bottles of water and the Coca-Cola stands, the rosaries and the little medallions which have all, according to the little cards attached to them, been dipped in the Jordan, form a thriving industry. They are saying: "It would be kind of you to buy," and it is not difficult to be kind at Bethabara. I remember a day when five priests belonging to five denominations led their flocks simultaneously to the water's edge, and they were all chanting or reciting, while each group pretended that the others did not exist.

The trouble is that no one really knows the site of the baptism. The Gospel of St. John says it took place "beyond the Jordan," which is not very helpful. There is no good reason to believe that it took place in the Jordan at all. The Pilgrim of Bordeaux, writing about A.D. 333 and therefore knowledgeable about the earliest traditions, says it took place "beyond the Jordan about five miles to the north of the Dead Sea." On the Madaba mosaic we can read the words "Bethabara of St. John the Baptist" near the mouth of the Dead Sea; we see a church standing a little way back from the river; and the mosaicist has used bright red cubes to emphasize the importance of the site. Nevertheless he was relying on inspired guesswork.

Although the site has very little to commend it historically, it is an enchanting place. Walk for five minutes along the shores of the Jordan among the willows and the tamarisks, and you come to a wide stretch of the river where there are no pilgrims, no booths, no picturesque Arabs waiting to be photographed. It is very quiet here. Birds are singing, and soon you grow accustomed to the singing of the river, which flows to its own music. Sometimes there is a sudden movement in the brakes. They say that gazelles, wild boars and cheetahs drink at the river, but I never saw them and doubt whether they come now. I saw a large fish, all silver and blue, gliding merrily downstream, little knowing that it had only a few more minutes to live. Soon it would enter the Dead Sea and die, and become mummified, and sink to the bottom encrusted with salt. The Madaba mosaic tells a different story. It shows a fish coming close to the Dead Sea and very sensibly turning back.

History flows around the river, but much of it remains unknown. There are twenty places along its shores which cry out to be excavated. At Tell es Saidiyeh, not far from Succoth, the University of Pennsylvania has been excavating a promising site that includes Bronze Age remains and the vestiges of a Greek temple; no one knows the original name of the town. The Old Testament provides a reasonably complete if not always accurate history of the Israelites, but we know little enough about the Amorites and Moabites and the other tribes which settled nearby. Their history is all mystery and confusion, and so it will remain until the archaeologists dredge up the evidence from beneath the soil.

Meanwhile the river flows on, strangely beautiful, mysteriously feminine, defying the desert, discreet and elusive. Compared with the real rivers, the Nile, the Euphrates, the Mississippi, it is scarcely a river at all. One of the headwater streams springs from the Cave of Baniyas, and there the Greeks built a small temple to Pan to celebrate their joy in its coming forth. They had chosen sensibly, for the river gives an impression of abundant joy throughout its length as it ripples gaily through an inhospitable land.

One day, driving from Jericho to Amman, I stopped the car at the bridge where the Jordan widens before it flows into the Dead Sea. Someone had told me there was a backflow from the Dead Sea and the last stretches of the Jordan were brackish. I hesitated for a moment because the taste of Dead Sea water is one of the most unpleasant imaginable, and there, under the bridge, where automobiles were roaring past on the darkening highway, I cupped my hands in the water. It was still sweet. I stood there for a while watching the fish going to their deaths, and the waving reeds, and the desolation of the Dead Sea, which was the color of lead, while the mountains of Moab were fading in the sky. No doubt all rivers fall into a salt sea, but it seemed strange that the Jordan should suffer this fate. It deserved better—so fresh, so living a thing deserved to feed into a fresh-water lake, not the Dead Sea where everything dies.

ISRAEL

COMING TO JERUSALEM

We live in an apocalyptic age: moonlight, the great cliffs, ourselves wandering on the edge of them. Once we lived on the sunlit plain, and the signposts were properly and accurately displayed, and there was reasonable shelter, and most men knew what to do with their lives. Now we are lucky if we can recognize our friends and succeed in standing upright on the cliff edge. A little wind could blow us over.

So I thought as I drove from the coast to Jerusalem, along that winding interminable road that seems to lead from the modern age into the most ancient past. Certainly there can be no city so modern as Tel Aviv and none so ancient as Jerusalem, the one so quick, so intolerant, so feverish, and the other so calm and serene with the wisdom of the ages. The truth was that Tel Aviv always frightened me. The spectacular marble hotels, the garish streets, the fierce traffic, the restless faces jarred on me, and I preferred the slower pace of Jerusalem, where people walked calmly and resolutely about the day's business. Always there was the sense of coming home—a quieter home. From the time of the Prophets people have spoken of the Ascent to Jerusalem, as though the very fact of climbing gave authority to the journey. Jerusalem the Golden, the City of Peace, holy and blessed above all other cities, was less than an hour away from Tel Aviv, and already we were outside time all together.

Time, in Jerusalem, is still biblical time. Elsewhere we race along on the circumference of the wheel, but in Jerusalem we are at the slow-moving hub of the wheel. The centuries pass, but nothing changes.

Buildings and temples which have long since vanished are restored by an act of the imagination. Calvary, Herod's Temple, the Rock of Abraham have all been cut down, recarved, partially destroyed, but there remains enough for the imagination to complete the whole. At the still center of the revolving wheel everything is fixed and unchangeable like the Pole Star.

Along that winding road there were still some relics of the 1947 war. A burned-out armored car lay on its side at a turning of the road, like the bones of an antediluvian monster, up-ended and obscene, stained with red rust and green fungus, crumbling as rocks crumble. Beyond it lay the bleak hills, savage and uninviting, offering so little promise of Jerusalem that you sometimes find yourself wondering whether in fact anything so improbable as Jerusalem could possibly lie at the end of the road. The ascent is cruel and nerve-wracking. The Anglo-Saxon pilgrim Saewulf, writing in A.D. 1102 shortly after the Crusaders had taken possession of Jerusalem, described that cruel journey vividly:

> We went up from Joppa to the city of Jerusalem, a journey of two days, by a mountainous road, very rough, and dangerous on account of the Saracens, who lie in wait in caves of the mountains to surprise the Christians, watching both day and night to surprise those less capable of resisting by the smallness of their company, or the weary, who may chance to lag behind their companions. At one moment you see them on every side; at another they are altogether invisible, as may be witnessed by everyone traveling there. Numbers of human bodies lie scattered on the way, and by the wayside, torn to pieces by wild beasts. Some may perhaps wonder why the bodies of Christians are allowed to remain unburied, but it is not surprising when we consider that there is not much earth on the hard rock to dig a grave; and if earth were not wanting, who would be so simple as to leave his company and go alone and dig a grave for a companion? Indeed, if he did so, he would rather be digging a grave for himself than for a dead man. For on that road not only the poor and the weak but the rich and strong are surrounded with perils; many are cut off by the Saracens, but more by heat and thirst; many perish by the want of drink, but more by too much drinking. We, however, with all our company reached the end of our journey.

So they did, arriving in Jerusalem in a state of exhaustion, after stepping carefully over the bodies of their fellow Christians. Saewulf was a cautious observer, and we can still feel the horror of the journey. Baldwin I, King of Jerusalem, commanded the Crusader army, ruling from his palace near David's tower, but he could not guarantee the safety of the pilgrims, who sometimes died miserably in sight of Jerusalem's golden gates.

We sang "Jerusalem the Golden," little knowing that the city was indeed golden. When at last you have come over the brow of the last hill, Jerusalem lies before you in all its small immensity, gold as the crust of well-baked bread.

THE HOLY SEPULCHRE

It was early in the evening and already dark when I reached the courtyard of the Church of the Holy Sepulchre, stepping down from the long covered street of cobblestones where the fly-specked shops were being shuttered for the night. There was a space of brilliant indigo blue sky over the courtyard, and I could hear the sharp rattle of the donkeys' hooves on the cobblestones. It was too late, I thought, to enter the church, but at least it was possible to see it from the outside by the light of the full moon, but the moon was too low to illuminate the strange building that rose against the shapeless sky suddenly fretted out by the immense scaffoldings, ropes, pulleys, ladders, heaps of masonry, which showed that the church was suffering one more of its many face-liftings. I was making my first visit to Jerusalem, and had no way of knowing what the church should have looked like at night. Tarpaulins hung across the sky, the courtyard smelled of brick dust and concrete, there were curious creaking and sucking noises made by the wind. Decidedly this small courtyard was not what I had expected for a church as spectacular and famous as this crowning basilica of all Christian churches.

I wandered for a while around the courtyard with its sour yeast smell of wet concrete. Every shadow concealed heaps of rubble, mortars, troughs, building implements, and it was obviously absurd to be wandering around in the darkness. A quick flash of light appeared as a door opened. A priest emerged, saw me, said: *"Fermato,"* and went on his way up the steps to the cobblestoned street. Then it was dark again, and I was still wandering about in this small, cluttered, unprepossessing courtyard, trying to make out the shape of the church.

What puzzled me was that it was so completely alien to anything I had expected. I thought I knew it well from books, but no one had ever told me that the approach was squalid and terribly wrong. There was no grand entrance way. The wind rose, and the tarpaulins began to wave and rustle with a curious flapping noise, black flags against a dark sky, and even when the moon rose high enough to throw some splinters of silvery light on all this confusion there was a sense of desolation.

I decided to try the door from which the priest had emerged, found it at last and stumbled into the church, which was unguarded and very quiet and very dark, with only a few altar lamps flickering. The church looked small from outside. Inside it was vast and cavernous. Huge shadows roamed across the walls and from somewhere came the sound of voices. It occurred to me that someone would soon come up and order me out of the building, but meanwhile here was a magnificent opportunity to see the church in the silence of the night, without people getting in the way. Now that I have seen it many times, at all hours of the day, I still prefer the memory of it in the near-darkness of that first night, the oil lamps winking and the visitors gone. At night the church becomes rock again.

Of course, the church has been rebuilt so often that it is almost without any logical shape. Originally there was a chapel built round the tomb, and another, a few yards away, around the rock of Golgotha, and still another around the place where St. Helena is supposed to have found the three crosses. Three centuries had elapsed since the death of Jesus when the Emperor Constantine ordered the construction of the three churches together with a baptistry and an *atrium,* an entrance hall entered from one of the main streets. Three hundred years later, in A.D. 614, the church was burned down by the Persians. It was partially rebuilt by Modestos, the *higoumenos* of the Convent of Theodosius, and destroyed again in A.D. 1009 by order of the mad Caliph Hakim. This time the destruction was nearly complete and the tomb itself appears to have been leveled to the ground. Thirty-three years later the Byzantine Emperor Constantine Monomachos built an enclosure around the site of the tomb and another around the site of Calvary. When the Crusaders entered Jerusalem on July 15, 1099, they found the church built by Constantine Monomachos in the Byzantine fashion and immediately decided to build a new church which would embrace the site of the tomb, Calvary and the Chapel of the Invention of the Cross. The church we see today is essentially the church of the Crusaders.

In the dim light it was easy to discern the edicule, the circular chapel built around the tomb, because it stands in isolation beneath the domed roof. It is small and squat, without charm, about the size of a poor peasant's hut, and is entered by a narrow passageway. Over the site of the tomb there was a blue-veined marble slab and an icon of a sorrowing Madonna. There was something about the interior of the edicule which suggested that the design had foundered because too many architects had been consulted, with the result that no one could come to any conclusion about the way it should be built, and they had left the matter to the least capable architect. The present edicule was not designed by the Crusaders; it was designed by a certain Comninos, a Greek from Mytilene, after a disastrous fire in 1808.

While the edicule, even in the darkness, resembled a rather gaudy pepperpot and was wholly out of place, the rest of the church was wonderfully fashioned, cavernous, with a narrow staircase leading up to Golgotha and a vast, theatrical staircase leading down to the Crypt of St. Helena. Chapel opened out into chapel. There were places where every inch of a wall glowed dull gold, and other places where the darkness was so intensely dark that I feared to fall into an abyss; and looking up, it sometimes seemed that black banners were drifting down from an invisible roof. Once, near the edicule, I encountered a small, black-gowned Armenian priest, who offered to lead me to the tomb. This was unfair; the outstretched fingers curled for *baksheesh;* he soon scurried away. I climbed the stone steps to Golgotha to find no one there, but voices could be heard nearby. Where they came from I never discovered; the church was full of echoes. The most happy moment was when I found myself peering into the darkness at the head of the stairway leading to the Crypt of St. Helena and then gingerly going down the steps toward the winking altar lights below. This stairway down into the depths was totally unexpected, for I had imagined there was only a small crypt, perhaps ten steps down, perhaps five. Instead there was a stairway fit for a king, for great processions, or for people to sit and watch a drama being performed below in the open space where an altar had been erected with an inscription saying it had been built at the orders of Ferdinandus Maximilianus Archid. Austri, the younger brother of the Emperor Franz Josef of the Austro-Hungarian Empire, and himself briefly the Emperor of Mexico.

And it is that unexpected stairway like an amphitheatre glimmering in the darkness, descending deeper and deeper into the heart of Jerusalem, that I remember most vividly when I think of the Church of the Holy Sepulchre, which is far more than a church and contains no vestiges of the sepulchre and perhaps no vestiges of Calvary, for the Persians and the mad Caliph Hakim had destroyed them so that nothing remained except the memory of them in this place, or near here, not very far away. What remained was neither a tomb nor a place of execution but the huge pit where St. Helena found, or believed she found, the three crosses, and this pit had been transformed into a processional highway.

Some days later, coming again to the church, I found this highway thronged with young French pilgrims, boys and girls, carrying candles and singing hymns, and as they came down the steps they formed a wave of light and a wave of full-throated song. In the glory of their coming it was possible to forget the preposterously ugly edicule and the gallery where the faithful were permitted to kneel down and dip their hands into the invisible socket which had perhaps held the crucifix, although all the historical evidence tended to show that the rock had long ago been leveled off. So I rejoiced in the processions and was bemused by the priests who said: "Here is the Column of Flagellation, here is the Stone of Unction, here Mary stood," and all the other things they said so lightly and with such an air of conviction. It was easier to believe the words spoken on Easter morning: "Why seek ye the living among the dead? He is not here."

THE STONES OF JERUSALEM

In those days I was drunk with Jerusalem, the splendor of the place, the golden and honey-colored stone, and the strange quivering light that beat up from the fierce Judaean hills. I think this drunkenness had very little to do with the holy relics, patiently examined and usually found wanting. I find it difficult to believe that anyone can possibly know the exact spot where Jesus was born, where he was crucified, and where he was entombed, and least of all was it possible to believe in the shapeless footprint in the Chapel of the Ascension. The stations of the Cross were equally imaginary, equally dubious. In the fourth and fifth centuries and right up into the Middle Ages the priests were busy labeling every stone in Jerusalem: "Here sat Ananias," "Here Peter heard the cockcrow," "Here Jesus looked back on Jerusalem," "This is the stone of the flagellation." It was the wildest kind of guesswork and would grow wilder in later centuries, when the cult of relics served to increase the wealth of many grave-robbers.

It seemed to me that holiness was not in the separate parts but in the whole. It was palpably present but you were no closer to it by dipping your hand into the socket in the rock which may once have supported the Cross. Holiness was the shining in the air; it was walking in the footsteps of the beloved; it was knowing that events that took place quietly were remembered and would have shattering effect; it was the certainty that life possessed a meaning, even if it could not be put into words and thoughts. Holiness lay in the knowledge that all life under the sun was sacramental. *Numen inest.* But the divine majesty was not something which had taken up its habitation in a church or temple; it was in the human heart. The earthly reflection of that majesty was represented in art, especially in sculpture, poetry, music and painting, and in places like Galilee and Jerusalem, Azraq and Rumm, Karnak and Saqqara, where the splendor was most palpable. There was a place called the Holy Land, but you could not say that any particular stone was more holy than another. You could not put a fence round a stone, and say: "It is holy up to here and beyond this point it loses its holiness." You could not say that north was more holy than south. Was the Pole Star more holy than the Pleiades? Holiness was not a substance, a face, a stone, a splinter of wood. It could not be isolated. It was more like the wind that moves across the wheat fields and turns the fields white.

There was a nun in the blue-domed Russian Church of St. Mary Magdalene on the slopes of Gethsemane who walked with me in the church gardens. She was about sixty, white-faced, moved slowly, said little, kept her head bent very low, and sometimes fluttered her hands in a way that was like saying farewell to the world. She spoke very gravely with long pauses, and there were moments when she stood quite still with her eyes closed. I asked whether she was well enough to come out, for I had heard that she had been ill, and she said that God had favored her, she was well again, she asked nothing except to be allowed to live a little while longer on this spot where Christ had suffered so greatly on behalf of sinful humanity. From this garden there was a wonderful view over Jerusalem, with the golden cupola of the Dome of the Rock gleaming a little below us, but she never looked up, saw nothing of the world around her. Then in the shadow of the pine trees, the blue domes rising behind her, she paused abruptly and pointed to some ancient stones forming part of a stairway breaking through the grass. They were chalky yellow, like loaves, smooth and well worn. She said: "Tread delicately here. On these very stones Christ walked on his way to be crucified."

"You are quite certain these are the very stones?"

"Of course," she answered, and half knelt to caress them. "The very ones."

"How do you know?"

"By the eyes of faith. You see, we are very privileged here. I pity all those who cannot walk in his footsteps."

Her fingers ran along the stones with a kind of abandonment. I had the feeling that these three stones were sacred to her and they were as smooth as loaves because she had caressed them so often.

I said, not intending to be cruel: "Judas also walked down these steps?"

The thought shocked her, her hand made a sudden lunging movement as though Judas had suddenly appeared before her, and her lips trembled violently. Then she grew very quiet, straightened herself, and walked toward a grove of pine trees. Finally she turned to me and said sternly: "It was very wrong of you to speak about Judas on Gethsemane."

I wandered about Jerusalem in a state of exaltation but also of incredulity that so many people should reverence so many rocks and stones. It was true that the stone of Jerusalem is honey-colored, fine-grained, and can be easily worked; but the worship of stones in the Semitic East has nothing to do with the beauty of stone. Stones, huge slabs of stone, were erected on high mountains to indicate the abiding presence of a god. We speak of the Rock of Ages, but every mountain is a rock of ages. What is meant by this peculiar fondness for rocks found all over the harsh, rocky landscape of Palestine and Jordan? The stones of Jerusalem were once relics that were bought and sold in the Middle Ages, and they are still worshiped. Each religion has its most sacred rock: the Wailing Wall of the Jews, the Calvary of the Christians, the Moslems' Dome of the Rock demand the worship of the faithful. Happily they are not very close together and the pilgrims do not get in each others' way.

I found no answer to the problem, and so I attempted to find an answer in a poem.

JERUSALEM

Night falls, Jerusalem sleeps, and the world ends.
And I am standing on Gethsemane amid the shadows
Of a city which is no city, a city drained of corporeal essence,
Being more and less than a city, being shrouded in darkness,
A place of darkness, invisible, intangible, a city at the
bottom of the ocean.
Nevertheless in the darkness the city is there, and the eye
grows accustomed
Slowly to the glimmering stones, to the faint light on the
sharp edges,

To that wild scattering of stones on a hill-top in the midst
of a desert.
And I ask myself: Is this darkness Jerusalem? Is this the
heart of the world?
Stone. Stone. Stone. Stone everywhere. Stone and
darkness.

O tiger of stone
O stone of the Annunciation
O stone of the Anointment
O stone of the Holy Sepulchre
O stone of Abraham
O stone of the temple
O stone of the heart
O stone of the rib cage
O stone of our sex
O stone of our brain
Is there no end to stone?

Strange how the worship of stones continued through the ages,
And stranger still the worship of the hollowed out rocks,
Sepulchres and tombs, caves, cairns, hollows, monuments
To the defeat of all life under the sun. Stone innumerable,
Cracked and bleached by the sun, pounded into powder.
Beyond all reckoning or reason we worship the holy stones:
Wherefore mortality holds us by a stone throat. On this
stone Jesus trod.
On this stone Jacob slept, seeing the angels ascending and
descending.
On this stone Abraham held the knife at Isaac's throat.
From this stone Muhammad rode his horse into Heaven.
This stone, and no other. This rock of ages.
And any child who plays with any stone
May find he is holding an inch of the Holy Sepulchre.

O tiger of stone
O stone of abasement
O stone of triumph
O stone of illumination
O stone of darkness
O seas of stone

O clouds of stone
O flowers of stone
O trees of stone
O days of stone
O nights of stone

So you may travel across the desert and see here and there
A little heap of stones recording that someone passed
                    before you,
For this is the habit in the desert. The wanderers want
                    to be remembered.
They write their names on the stones, they scribble blood on
                    the stones, make some mark,
Then stand for a while gazing at their handiwork before
                    passing on
To the liquid mirage of the horizon, knowing they are not
                    entirely forgotten.
They have spoken, the stones have mouths, the stones speak
                    for them:
For the stones are hungry to take on the form of human flesh,
Of animals, of tigers, even of birds: they go in search of
                    the living.
Mouths they have, eyes also, they watch the passing of the
                    seasons.
The sun climbs up the stone in the morning and descends in
                    the evening,
And the stone is made holy by the shadow of everyone who
                    passes by.
          O stone of God
          O stone of the Resurrection
          O stone of the Wailing Wall
          O stone of the Assassination
          O stone of our eyes
          O stone of our mouths
          O stone of our hearts
          O stone of our loves
          O stone of Jerusalem

THE ARCHAEOLOGIST

She had carved and sliced into old Jerusalem, cut trenches, bored through the rock, managed her teams of laborers as though she was Pharaoh, and discovered what no one had expected to discover: that the city of David covered only an area of ten acres and was in fact not a city but a small village clinging to the side of a mountain.

In Jerusalem Dr. Kathleen Kenyon was a power to be reckoned with. She was an institution. I thought of her with that peculiar reverence which is reserved for those rare people who have been transformed into legend and are therefore unreachable. In the history of archaeology she ranks with Dr. Flinders Petrie and Auguste Mariette Pasha, digging where no one had ever thought to dig before and always finding treasure. The treasure, a year's dig, lay on the trestle tables, waiting to be examined by the Inspector-General of Antiquities. There were no gold cups, no splendid jewel-encrusted sarcophagi, no jewelry at all except for a few blue beads that may have come from Egypt. The treasure consisted of potsherds, broken figurines, the detritus of ancient trash-heaps. A smashed water jug, now cunningly put together, was her special favorite.

She came into the room like a ship in full sail, fat and jolly, a cigarette at the corner of her lips. She was very English, very crisp, very self-assured. She smoked incessantly and would find herself lighting a new cigarette before she had finished the last. It appeared that the ship in full sail was also equipped with an auxiliary engine; and sometimes the ship and all the blue sail-cloth vanished in tumultuous clouds of smoke.

"In the first place we have come down to bedrock," she said. "We can never know any more about David's city than we know now. No signs of wealth and power, no weapons, no jewelry, or so little that it scarcely counts. They were hardy peasants and shepherds, and had no more possessions than you would expect from a pastoral people. No substantial buildings, no temples, nothing that could remotely resemble a palace. In the second place they quickly transformed the Jebusite city into a fortress. They were concerned to strengthen their position—this above all. They had taken Mount Ophel and were absolutely determined to hang on to it."

In the last years of the eleventh century B.C. the Israelites under Saul were being heavily pressed by the Philistines. Saul threw himself on his sword to avoid being slain by the Philistine archers; David, the boy king, anointed at Hebron, took the lesson to heart and taught his people the use of the bow. But he did not win his new kingdom by the bow. His small and ragged army arrived at the foot of Mount Ophel to be greeted by the Jebusites who called down from the ramparts: "You shall not come in here but the blind and the lame shall prevent you." Smarting, David set about conquering it in other ways. There was a *sinnor*, a water-funnel, cut into the rock and leading to the fountain pool below. Water buckets were let down and the pure water came up through the funnel. "And David said on that day, Whosoever getteth up the gutter, and smiteth the Jebusites, and the lame and the blind, that are hated of David's soul, he shall be chief and captain." And then, according to the *Book of Chronicles*, Joab, his nephew, "went first up and was chief."

The tiny community of Jebusites gave way to the tiny community of David, and the events of one day changed the course of history.

If Mount Ophel had not been captured by David, then the kingdom of Israel, divided and weakened by ancestral quarrels, might have sunk without a trace. The Law of Moses would have perished, Christianity would not have emerged, and there would have been no Islam. All that had gone before, all the battles and skirmishes and wanderings, were as nothing compared to this decisive event. In the beginning there was this kingdom covering an area of ten acres. Out of it there would grow soaring legends and mythologies and rival faiths, dreams and visions, vast palaces and temples, and eternal conflicts.

David enlarged his frontiers. Once again the shepherd king used guile.

A vision commanded him to buy the threshing floor of Araunah the Jebusite which stood above Ophel and to erect the altar around which his son Solomon built the Temple. On this rock, called Mount Moriah, the legends gathered like flocks of many-colored birds, and even the most improbable legends, the most wry-headed birds of all, alighted and spread their wings to shelter their fledglings. Never have so many legends gathered on a single spot. Here Adam was created from a spoonful of dust, here Cain slew Abel, here Noah prayed before the flood, here Abraham was about to offer up his son Isaac until God relented and permitted him instead to sacrifice a lamb caught in a thicket, and from here Muhammad's horse, al-Buraq, the Lightning Flash, bore the Prophet to heaven. The threshing floor became the foundation stone of the world and the place of the Last Judgment.

So the legends accumulated, one legend inviting another, one flock of many colored birds inviting another flock. If it was beyond reason that the world's beginnings and endings must all take place in Araunah's farmyard, it was not beyond faith.

The secret, if there is one, lies with David and his son Solomon, who was born to Bathsheba, whose lawful husband David sent to his death. The Jews ascribed all their psalms to David. What is certain is that he had the poetic spirit, the capacity for wild improvisation, the vision of God. Legends accumulated around him; he thrived on them; he poured out new legends like a man scattering grain in the plowed fields. He was the visionary, the contemplative. His son had the sinewy feeling for things, for power, for earth. He thirsted after glory, whereas David thirsted after righteousness. The combination of the visionary and the man of lusty ambitions is an especially potent one, and likely to be explosive. Out of the threshing floor emerged Solomon's temple, which was quite small, scarcely a hundred feet wide, wonderfully constructed by Phoenician workmen out of gold, ivory, bronze and stone, and then, nearly a thousand years later, the vast magnificence of Herod's sumptuous temple. And none of this would have happened if Araunah had not sold the threshing floor for six hundred shekels of gold.

Even now, though Kathleen Kenyon has uncovered all that remains of David's city, so that we know its exact dimensions, and the position of the gates, the towers and the approaches, we know very little about it. On the trestle tables, wearing their ancient dust like a garment, the little clay animals rested on broken feet and here too were the heavily ringletted women with their hands cupped to their breasts, votive offerings to the Jebusite goddess of fertility. They were crudely fashioned, and passionless, though their eyes glared. Ancient Jerusalem had revealed its secrets: they were pitiably few.

Blue clouds of cigarette smoke drifted over the tables, while the archaeologist marched up and down between them. Each relic was numbered, photographed, entered into the account book with a record of exactly where it was found, on what level, in what condition. A year's work had come to an end, and the fruits of it were on display in this upstairs room in the British School of Archaeology. Kathleen Kenyon observed them anxiously, like a general observing new recruits who did not look as though they would make good soldiers or bring much renown to the nation.

"What happens now?" I asked hopefully, for it seemed inconceivable that all these objects were being displayed for my benefit.

"What happens is the division of the spoils. The Director General of Antiquities will take what he wants, whatever is important to him. We shall take the rest. We don't know what he wants. It's ghastly, this waiting around. He's coming at four o'clock."

There was another barrage of cigarette smoke.

"Can he take all of it?"

"Yes, if he wants to, but of course he won't. If we had discovered a hoard of jewels, he might take all of it, and properly so, because it belongs here. We haven't discovered anything earth-shattering, and he will probably take just a few pots. What time is it?"

"Fifteen minutes past two."

"Damn the waiting!"

She stubbed out a cigarette and lit another. For a while she talked about Jericho, where she had cut deep trenches revealing settlements that went back to the eighth millennium B.C., making it the oldest city in the world, and laughed, and tried not to think about the division of the spoils. At Jericho, above the first signs of human habitation, she found five cities, and the fourth appears to have been the one conquered by Joshua. Here there were double walls nearly thirty feet thick, and there was considerable evidence that there had been an earthquake followed by a fire. It appeared that Joshua's arrival outside Jericho coincided with an earthquake which destroyed the impregnable walls. Trumpets sounded with the roar of an earthquake, and the city fell.

She waved her arms, swept Jericho away, darted toward a potsherd that suddenly attracted her attention, and was off again on a long disquisition on potsherds, their care and maintenance, so that you might have thought they were small animals that needed to be fed regularly and put to bed at night. The telephone rang. Dust rose. Cities fell. In the excitement the room with the trestle tables seemed to wheel round, tilt and upend itself; the treasures of David's city were cascading on the floor. In the midst of all the turmoil Dr. Kathleen Kenyon, doyen of archaeologists, came sailing like a huge blue-sailed galleon, in a cloud of blue smoke and firing broadsides from all her guns.

THE DOME OF THE ROCK

Wherever you are in Jerusalem, you can take your bearings by the dazzling golden Dome of the Rock, which is so perfectly proportioned that it must be accounted the single most beautiful building in the world. It was begun by Abd al-Malik in A.D. 687 and completed four years later, and what we see today is virtually the same building as it left the hands of his builders. It is both the oldest and the most splendid building in Jerusalem.

The dome enshrines a rock on a site known to the Moslems as the Haram al-Sharif, the Noble Sanctuary. It is a very ordinary rock in appearance with some craggy edges and much scoring, but in its honor Abd al-Malik erected a sumptuous temple thickly adorned with mosaics and marble columns, and there is some evidence that Syrian Christians worked on the mosaics and perhaps on the architectural design. At all costs Abd al-Malik was determined to build a temple more sumptuous than any existing temple in Palestine, and succeeded beyond all expectation.

Today the rock has something of the appearance of a small petrified lake set in a richly colored tropical forest. The light from stained glass windows and snow-white columns, from bronze beams and glittering sheets of mosaic falls on it, but it does not reflect the light. Jerusalem stone, when it is newly carved, has a rich golden luxuriance, like the golden crusts of newly baked bread, but this rock has only a shadowy greyness. So old, so used, so worn, it is fading away into the quiet grayness of age, lost beneath the gleaming magnificence of its setting.

For the Haram al-Sharif is no more than the setting of the rock, as a ring offers a setting for a precious stone. All this magnificence is displayed to honor the barren rock, whose history is so ancient that it seems to go back to the time when the earth was still shrouded in the mists of creation. Here the priest-king Melchizedek offered sacrifice, and here Abraham led Isaac and would have sacrificed him if an angel had not come from heaven and pointed to a ram caught in a thicket. Here Araunah the Jebusite threshed his corn and winnowed it until David came from nearby Zion and bought the rock and the Jebusite's oxen for fifty shekels of silver and built an altar to Jehovah, which Solomon converted into a temple, which the Chaldeans burned. Then Zerubbabel built a second temple after the return of the Jews from exile, and this temple, though twice profaned and desecrated, survived intact for nearly five hundred years until Herod the Great tore it down and rebuilt it more to his liking. Under Zerubbabel as under Herod, the rock was the altar of sacrifice, and the blood of the slaughtered beasts was dashed into the gaping hole which leads into the cavern where Araunah once stored his corn.

A million beasts were slaughtered here in the open air, for the rock was uncovered. It stood in the court of the priests only a few steps away from the Holy of Holies. The blood, we are told, was strewn over the rock in the form of the Greek letter gamma Γ, and even now we can make out the three corners, corresponding to the three points of the compass, where the blood was strewn. Here the paschal lamb was sacrificed, and here were offered up the shewbread, the first sheaves of Passover and the loaves of Pentecost. The unhewn rock gleamed red with blood or white with the water which cleansed the blood away.

The priests officiated in gold and blue vestments, jeweled and mitred, chanting the praises of God in deep and resonant voices. They arose in the grey mornings, watching for the first light that dawned on Hebron before lifting their heavy skirts and walking up the steps to the rock, where God was present. They sang joyfully, the embroidered bells and pomegranates testifying to a joyous faith as they sacrificed at the rock of atonement which was also the rock of their salvation.

When Titus conquered Jerusalem in A.D. 70, the temple was destroyed stone by stone until it was no more than smoking rubble. Never again would the Jews worship there. Hadrian remembered that the place was sacred and built on the site a temple to Venus and himself. When the Christian emperors came to power in Constantinople, the temple of Venus vanished.

For three centuries the weeds grew among the rubble; the refuse of all

Jerusalem was poured on the desolate place; and when the Caliph Umar captured Jerusalem in A.D. 638 he had to crawl on his hands and knees through the choked gates to find the rock from which according to Islamic tradition Muhammad had flown to heaven on Buraq, the winged horse with an angel's face. The rock that was once so hallowed now rested beneath a mountain of filth and ordure. Providentially there came three heavy showers of rain, and the rock emerged into the sunlight without human help. With his own hands the Caliph helped to build a little wooden shrine over the rock. Some fifty years later the Umayyad Caliph Abd al-Malik ibn Marwan built the great golden-domed shrine we see today.

For the Umayyad Caliph, who poured into the decoration of the shrine all the tribute he received from Egypt during seven years, the possession of the small naked rock signified his chief claim to the affection and loyalty of the faithful, and he announced that henceforth it was no longer necessary to make pilgrimages to Mecca; it was enough that the faithful should journey to Jerusalem. But only the very privileged were permitted to set eyes on the rock, for he put up a lattice screen of ebony covered with curtains of thick brocade. Sacred objects must be veiled and kept from sight. Once again the rock became invisible.

It was during this period that the sacred relics were collected and placed in the shrine—the battle flag of Umar, two hairs from the beard of the Prophet, the horn of Abraham's ram and the imperial crown of the Persian emperor Chosroes. The shrine was a reliquary, and could contain as many relics as the reigning Caliph desired. A mysterious slab of grey-veined marble inset with nineteen golden nails was said to have been placed there by Muhammad. Visitors were told that they must walk carefully when they approached it, lest the nails fall out and centuries vanish. Time would be convulsed by the dropping of a nail.

In fact the Caliph had hoped that the holy rock of Jerusalem would take the place of the Kaaba in Mecca not only as a place of pilgrimage but as the supreme mystery of the Islamic faith; and from his palace in Damascus the law went out commanding that worship be paid to the rock. The authentic traditions were overlaid with new and more fabulous legends. A new history was given to the rock. It was said that Moses had always prayed in the direction of the rock, and that when Muhammad made his Night Ascension to heaven, the rock rose with him and was left hovering in the air, detached from the earth. From the cave beneath the rock there issued the four rivers of Paradise—Sihon, Gihon, the Euphrates and the Nile, and in this same cave the dead met twice a year to worship God. Once the rock was twelve miles high and its shadow had fallen over Jericho; above it a brilliant ruby gleamed, and this same ruby, transformed into white coral, would become the throne of God on the Day of Judgment. Some ancient Jewish legends and traditions lingered on. Like the Jews, the Arabs believed that the rock was thirty-six miles from heaven, and they followed the ancient Jewish priests by insisting that those who walked around it must keep it always on the right.

The Arab imagination lingered over the rock, continually embellishing it with more and more magnificence. But where the Jews regarded it as quivering with life and movement, streaming with the blood of sacrificial offerings, the Arabs regarded it with all the more delight because it was naked and austere. No services were performed on the rock, no sacrifices were offered. The very barrenness of the rock served to enflame their imaginations, and they gloried in its emptiness, its silence, its perfect loneliness.

For four centuries the Moslems held Jerusalem. In the hot summer of 1099 the Crusaders armed with battering-rams and siege towers broke into the city. The Dome of the Rock fell to the armies of Tancred and Raymond Count of Toulouse. Some of the defenders, with their wives and children, took refuge on the low roof, and we are told by the chronicler that Tancred, moved by a sudden spirit of pity, "sent them his banners," meaning that they were allowed to go free. But no pity was shown to the defenders guarding the rock, for Daimbert of Pisa, the religious leader of the Crusade, reported to the Pope that the Crusaders rode in the blood of Moslems up to the knees of their horses in the *templum Salomonis*, the temple of Solomon. In the eyes of the Crusaders the shrine built by Caliph Abd al-Malik was the very temple of Solomon, which had survived through the centuries. When the Dome of the Rock fell into the hands of the Crusaders, they gave it a new name. It became *templum Domini*, the temple of the Lord.

The Crusaders changed little. The Arabic inscriptions around the drum of the dome were left unharmed. They tore down the curtains of heavy brocade and removed the ivory lattice, setting up instead a fence of gilded wrought-iron spears to signify their determination to protect the rock by force of arms. They set up a marble altar on the rock, and then because so many pilgrims were chipping fragments of rock to take away as relics, they covered it with marble sheeting. Once more the rock was invisible. A new altar was built, masses were said daily, an abbot ruled over the new foundation. The *templum Domini* was regarded with the same veneration as the Holy Sepulchre, for Baldwin I placed them side by side on his coins. The Templars carved the Dome of the Rock on their seals, and the Temple in London and many other circular shrines built all over Europe served to commemorate the *templum Domini*, believed to be the authentic temple of Solomon, unchanged and now at last in the possession of the followers of Christ, Solomon's successor.

An Arab historian, Al-Harawi, who visited Jerusalem in 1173, noticed that the great door was decorated with an image of Christ in hammered gold and studded with jewels. Solomon, he says, was remembered in the cave below, where a painting of him greeted the worshiper as he walked down the steps. It appears that Solomon had been relegated to the depths. Christ reigned above the rock, Solomon in the darkness beneath.

Just as the Jews saw the rock as the altar of the holocaust forever replenishing the earth and sustaining the faith, just as the Moslems saw it as the visible sign of Muhammad's power and as the stepping stone to heaven, so the Christians regarded it from their own special point of view. On the rock of Calvary Christ's life on earth had ended; on the rock of the Temple many of the most important acts of his ministry had taken place. Here Christ delivered his sermons, raised up the woman who committed adultery, and drove out the money-changers. Here he had come at the end of his triumphal procession to Jerusalem to announce the new law and the forthcoming destruction of the Temple. His footprint could be seen on the rock, and all history revolved around that point in space where he had stood.

Sir John Maundeville, who knew the Holy Land even if he never traveled through the deserts and cities of Asia which he claimed to have visited, tells us what the rock meant to him, or what he thought it meant to him. Nearly every event in sacred history had been enacted upon it. The rock indeed resembled a translucent crystal and if one peered into it one would see all the priests and saints congregated there, simultaneously performing their acts of blessedness:

And Jacob was sleeping upon that rock when he saw the angels go up and down by a ladder, and he said "Surely the Lord is in this place and I knew it not." And there an angel held Jacob still, and changed his name, and called him Israel. And in that same place David saw the angel that smote the people with a sword, and put it up bloody in the sheath. And St. Simeon was on that same rock when he received Our Lord into the Temple. On that rock Our Lord preached frequently to the people, and out of that same Temple Our Lord drove the buyers and sellers. Upon that rock also Our Lord set him when the Jews would have stoned him, and the rock clave in two, and in that cleft was Our Lord hid. And there came down a Star and gave him light, and upon that rock Our Lady sat and learned her Psalter, and there Our Lord forgave the woman her sins that was found in adultery. And there Our Lord was circumcised, and there the angel gave tidings to Zacharias of the birth of St. John the Baptist, his son; and there first Melchisedek offered bread and wine to Our Lord in token of the sacrament that was to come, and there David fell down praying to Our Lord and to the angel that smote the people, that he would have mercy on him and on the people, and Our Lord heard his prayer, and therefore would he make the Temple in that place, but the Lord forbade him by an angel because he had done treason, when he caused Uriah the worthy knight to be slain, to have Bathsheba as his wife, and therefore all the materials he had collected for the building of the Temple he gave to Solomon his son, and he built it.

So it goes on, that vast catalogue of all the great events of human history that took place on the rock. Here Adam was born, David sinned, Solomon built his Temple, Christ overturned the tables of the money-changers and vanished into the rock when he was threatened by the Jews, and from here Muhammad ascended to heaven. The rock is a magic ring. Turn it, and with every turn a new vision is conjured up. But the rather sinister grotto under the rock resembles a small prison cell, the lights are dim, the world closes in, and you escape from it as quickly as you can. According to the Moslems the souls of the dead can be heard moaning beneath the floor of the grotto, and Moslem women are not supposed to enter it for fear that they might converse with the dead.

A rock around which surrealist fantasies have accumulated over the centuries! Nothing in the least remarkable about that pitted, shapeless slab. Yet, as though it was the most valuable jewel of the world, it has been given a setting which is miraculously beautiful, colored by the shimmering mosaics of the dome, filled with rainbow colored lights, so that you have the feeling of being in Paradise, which is precisely the intention of the builders. Thus the Dome of the Rock, which derives ultimately from the round fourth-century Church of Santa Constanza in Rome built to contain the tomb of Constantia, the daughter of the Emperor Constantine, becomes at last the most visionary of objects, and a man may be drunk with Paradise long before he enters it.

There are no long faces in the Dome of the Rock; people talk to one another; children romp; the fat and jolly mullah in charge raises no objection if you ask permission to lie at full length on the floor to admire the blaze of mosaics, golden and yellow and orange, on the curved ceiling. There are thick carpets all brightly colored, an air of festivity, and if the mullah approves of you, he will show you a silver tube which contains some hairs from Muhammad's beard, the only other relic of importance in the entire building. Such things, of course, must be taken on trust. In the Great Mosque at Delhi I was once shown three hairs from Muhammad's beard which, when held up to the light, were scarlet. Red-bearded Muhammad? But Muhammad seemed strangely absent in the Dome of the Rock. Here, as you walk around the rock, you are conscious only of the wheeling colors, the sunbursts, the joy of life, and the absolute perfection of a building built thirteen centuries ago.

THE TOMB OF ABRAHAM

One place I particularly wanted to see was Hebron, with its *haram,* or sacred enclosure, built over the tomb of Abraham. The town was one of the oldest in the world, for if *The Book of Numbers* could be trusted on numerical matters, it was seven years older than Tanis, the very ancient capital of Lower Egypt. I knew that Abraham had bought from Ephron the Hittite the cave of Machpelah for his family sepulchre and was buried there with Isaac, Jacob, Sarah, Rebecca and Leah, and that it was once the capital of David. Absalom made it the headquarters of his rebellion, and in time Justinian built a church there, and later the Crusaders built an even greater church, which the Arabs transformed into a mosque. But what I knew most of all was that the dark syllables of Machpelah were strangely haunting, sounding as old as Abraham.

So I went there, wandering through the busy town to the temple-church-mosque constructed by Christians, Moslems and Jews—the huge stone courses which form the foundation of the *haram* were built by Herod—and found what appeared to be a fortress reached by a giant flight of steps; and inside, in the white unshadowed light, a strange vacuum. It was not in the least what I expected. From Abraham sprang Ishmael, the father of the Arab race, and Jacob, the father of the Jews. Hence its sanctity. More especially: before Abraham there were gods in plenty; only with Abraham there came the one God.

So one finds oneself walking very slowly among the cenotaphs, not knowing where to turn, confused and oppressed by the heaviness of the

147

air, the utter stillness of the place, the tawdry decoration, the ticking of the grandfather clock. There is no center, no focus, nowhere where the eye can rest. There are six cenotaphs and a marble grating under a cupola, and the rest is empty space. The visible objects in the *haram* are so arranged that they do not relate to one another. It is as though quite deliberately the architects had taken care that the building should give precisely this impression. In all this the *haram* is unlike the Dome of the Rock, which is designed to please. When Moslems enter that enchanted circle their faces light up and they are glad, for it is impossible not to be made glad by those dancing colors. But here all color has been drained away. Everything is sombre, dull, lifeless, so that you find yourself thinking of an abandoned railroad station. The *haram* is not intended to please. Instead, it inspires fear.

There is nothing like it anywhere else in the Moslem world. Many accidents have come together to produce a building so conspicuously desolate, so cold, so cruel, so awe-inspiring. The Herodian temple must have been bright with color, and the Crusaders' church must have had stained glass windows, a nave, transepts, an altar. The worshiper would have been at peace with himself, for his eyes would have been led from one sacred object to another, and in his explorations there would be purpose and direction. But here in the *haram* you are not asked to explore shapes and colors. The visible world is thrust away; death is everywhere. Even the elaborate pulpit, dulled with age, carries its cargo of death, for on this pulpit, made originally for a shrine in Ascalon, the head of Hussayn, the grandson of the Prophet, was laid. Death wanders carefree through these courts. It has taken up its abode here as surely as in a graveyard: only here it is more imperial, more august, and more demanding.

Imagine a romanesque church with vaulted ceiling and pointed windows, with here and there traces of its former magnificence, and then set within it immense cenotaphs heavy as lead, with straight sides and triangular roofs eight feet high, anchored to the marble floor, unmovable. The cenotaphs, if they had been a little smaller or if they had been placed closer to the wall, might have achieved some relationship with the building. In fact they remain totally unrelated, and they seem to have entered the place by the exercise of brute power. All the normal graces of Islamic design are absent. There is no delicate maneuvering of color, no hint of

Jerusalem

The Judaean Desert

The Road to Jerusalem

The High Priest of the Samaritans

The Tremore at Nazareth

The Sea of Galilee

The Dome of the Rock

The Dome of the Rock

a paradise to come. The world has come to an end among the dead dark rocks and the ghostly caves.

I remember thinking that I would never escape from this sanctuary, that anyone who ever enters it becomes its perpetual prisoner. In subtle ways everything conspires to root you to the floor; at most you can shuffle slowly from one wall to the other. Always you are reminded that the mystery is elsewhere and cannot be expressed: it lies in the cave below, gloomy and dreadful beyond belief, remote and unreachable, though it is only a few inches below your feet.

For many, many centuries the cave has been inspiring fear. An eighth-century Arab traveler, Abu Bekr el Eskafy, has left a record of his first and only attempt to penetrate the mystery. He took careful precautions, arranging to enter the cave on a winter day when there was no one about. He wrote:

> Because I was a well-known benefactor of the sanctuary, the guardian of the place agreed to let me enter the cave. He accordingly chose a day when there was a heavy downfall of snow and the cold weather prevented the pilgrims from coming. We stole into the sanctuary—myself, the guardian, and several workmen. The workmen lifted up the flagstone which covered the entrance to the cave. With a lamp in his hand, the guardian led me down a staircase with seventy-two steps. There I beheld a huge black slab on which there lay the body of Isaac, face upward. A full green cloth covered the body, and his long white beard was spread over the cloth. On two other slabs lay the bodies of Abraham and Jacob, their hair and beards spread out above the cloths. The guardian approached a wall in the cave, and I too drew near to look over his shoulder. At that moment a voice cried: Go from the *haram!* We fell down unconscious, and when we revived, we made our way back to the sanctuary.

Abu Bekr el Eskafy's account of his brief visit to the cave of Machpelah has generally been derided. Those mysterious voices issuing out of the mouths of caverns were only too familiar, for very similar stories were told about other attempts to enter sacred places. But there is at least a possibility that he was reporting accurately what he saw, or thought he saw. The white streaming beards of the patriarchs might have been the reflection of the lamp on polished black stone, and the voice crying out in the darkness might have come from one of the panic-stricken workmen. The seventy-two steps, the three black slabs, the lifted flagstone, even the green cloth suggest that he was observing accurately. He gives the impression of a man trying to tell the truth, however incredible it might appear.

More than three hundred and fifty years pass before we hear of another journey into the cave. Hebron fell to the Crusaders in 1099, and the old shrine built by Justinian on the stone courses laid by Herod the Great was now rebuilt with a narthex and three great naves. No attempt was made to enter the cave, and its existence seems to have been forgotten. On a hot summer day a monk who had been working in the scriptorium decided to rest from the heat by lying on the cool flagstones of the shrine, and in so doing he set in motion a series of events that led to the discovery of the bones of the patriarchs.

The account of the discovery was written in barbarous Crusader Latin by an Augustinian canon who heard it from the lips of those who took part. Here is his story:

> In the twenty-first year of the Franks' reign, a certain Rainier of pious memory was the prior in Hebron. Among those who came to serve God under his tutelage were Odon and Arnulf from whom I heard this story. These three men had each begged God to grant them a favor which he had refused to many others. At last God listened to their plea.
>
> It so happened one afternoon in June, while the Canons Regular were taking their customary siesta, that a monk who had been laboring in the scriptorium took refuge from the heat inside the church. He lay down on the flagstones beside one of the cenotaphs. Through a crevice in the stones there came a gentle current of fresh air. The monk began to throw pebbles through the opening, and on hearing them fall he concluded there must be a cavern or cistern below. He found a stick, fastened a string to it, and attached a leaden weight to the string. Then he lowered it to the floor of the cavern, which he found to be eleven elbows in depth. At this time the prior was attending to some affairs in Jerusalem.
>
> When the monks had arisen and chanted Nones, our monk told them about his discovery. They at once suspected that he had found the double cave of Machpelah. Two or three days were spent in prayers to God and in preparing cutting tools, for the rocks were solid and it would be difficult for iron tools to penetrate them. When everything was prepared, the monks agreed unanimously to begin work, and the superintendent, Baldwin, gave his approval. So they set to work in the name of the Blessed Trinity, not without some trepidation.
>
> After three days of strenuous labor they finished drilling through the rock

and were able to lift it. They found they were at the opening of the cavern. They were all anxious to enter the cavern, but there was room only for one of them. So it was decided that the oldest monk, who had also been longest in the monastery, should be permitted to go; and they reasoned that because he was, as it were, the father of all the rest, he would be more likely to discover the patriarchs of so many peoples. The old monk readily agreed to go, and was let down into the cavern. He could however find no way out of the place and asked to be lifted up.

On the following day Arnulf was let down into the cavern. He was carrying a candle. He looked around in perplexity, trying to make out the general configuration of the place. The walls of the cavern were so well joined together that they seemed to be carved from a single slab of stone, and the general shape followed that of the church above. He was at a loss and very perplexed because he was unable to find another passageway. But being a practical man of affairs, he took heart, seized a hammer, and began to tap the wall, listening for a hollow sound. At last he discovered what he was searching for.

With renewed hope he ordered others to come down and help him open the passageway. Four days passed before they were able to remove the rock. Behind it they found a large conduit, now dried up, eleven feet high, seventeen feet long, and a foot wide. They were all amazed by the fact that the walls of the narrow passageway were composed of squared blocks as carefully hewn as the walls of the church above. Arnulf was determined to find the relics and began to tap the walls. When he found another hollow sound, he urged them all to make a passage through the rock. Time passed —altogether it took four days to break through the rock. Then they found a round chapel which could hold thirty people, with an entrance blocked by a single slab of rock. Seeing this, the monks wept for joy and sang God's praises, but did not dare to enter the chapel, being sure the relics were inside. They waited for the prior to return, and when he came, they told him everything that had happened. He was in fact overjoyed by the news, regretting only that he had not been there from the beginning.

On that day there was a convocation of the monks, at which it was decided that immediately after the siesta and the chanting of Nones they would all enter the basilica below. Once there, they would make a thorough examination of the place to prepare for further action. Accordingly at the appointed hour they entered the cavern, rolled back the rock and entered the round chapel, but failed to find what they were looking for. While the monks were gazing round the shrine in amazement, for one does not expect to come upon such rooms underground, and while some of them closely examined the walls in the hope of finding an exit, Arnulf returned and set about examining the entrance. After some careful scrutiny of the light-colored rock, he found a wedge-shaped stone, and ordered it removed. Then he found the entrance to the second cavern, and with tears of joy everyone gave thanks to God.

On June 25 the prior ordered Arnulf, out of obedience and penance, to enter the second cavern, because he had done the most work in this endeavour. In this way he would bring the affair to a successful conclusion. Arnulf did not delay for a moment. Taking a candle, he blessed himself, chanted the *Kyrie* in a loud voice, and entered the cavern with some trepidation. And thinking that Baldwin, the superintendent of the monastery, might suspect that there was a treasure of gold or silver hidden in this place, he begged the prior to permit Baldwin to go with him. The request was granted, and Baldwin agreed to go, but the moment he entered the cavern he was overcome by terror and immediately withdrew.

Arnulf made his way through the cavern searching for bones, but he found nothing except earth dyed the color of blood. He then left the cavern and reported on what he had seen. Everyone was disappointed. The monks then left the cave. On the following day the prior urged Arnulf to examine the cavern once more and to make some careful excavations. Thereupon Arnulf obediently set out, taking a staff with him. Once more he entered the cavern, and began to dig up the earth. At last he came upon the bones of the saintly Jacob (although at the time he was unaware whose bones they were), and gathered them together. Then he discovered the entrance of another cave near the skull of Jacob. He cleared a passage and went within, and discovered the remains of Abraham, which were sealed, and at his feet the bones of Isaac. Some believe that all these relics were found in a single cave, but it is not so. The relics of Abraham and Isaac were discovered in an inner cave, while those of Jacob were found in an outer cave.

Arnulf had found a marvelous treasure beyond price. He hurried out of the cavern and told the prior and the monks that he had indeed discovered the remains of the venerable patriarchs. Thereupon they all praised God for what He had done. Arnulf washed the sacred relics in water and wine, and then set them on separate wooden boards prepared for the occasion, and went away. And all the others went away except the prior who sealed the entrance so that no man should enter the cavern unless he had given his authorization.

On the following day a handful of monks went down to pray and found several inscriptions on the stone at the right (of the cave mouth), but were unable to read them, and when they drew back the stone, they found nothing except earth. Assuming that the stone had been placed there for a very good reason, they dug to the left and found fifteen earthen pots filled with bones. But they were unable to learn anything about these relics. They must have been the bones of some Hebrew leaders.

When all this had taken place, the prior journeyed to Jerusalem to inform the Patriarch Garmund about the things that had come to pass and he went on to invite the Patriarch to Hebron that he might venerate the relics. The Patriarch promised to come, but failed to keep his word. And when the prior realized that he would not come, then he prepared a sacred ceremony of his own. A vast crowd of pilgrims came from Jerusalem and the neighboring places for the sacred rites which were held on October 6. The priests sang the *Te Deum* and the prior in solemn procession offered the relics for veneration.

The twelfth-century Augustinian monk who wrote this account of the discovery of the relics of Abraham, Isaac and Jacob was a man with an acute sense of story-telling. He never falters, never loses the thread. Three men who had actively taken part in the excavations had told him what happened at considerable length, and he had evidently checked and cross-checked their stories. He leaves out much we would like to know. We would like to know more about the dimensions of the caves, and how the bones were identified, and exactly what was done with them, and on these matters he is resolutely silent. But he is wonderfully skilled in suggesting the excitement of the discovery, the hesitations and uncertainties of the quest, and the moments of terror.

From the monk's description it is possible to imagine the ground plan of the caves. The exact positions of three entrances from the *haram* are known, and from time to time the Moslem imams in charge of the caves have given out brief but significant clues. One entrance lies to the left of the minbar on the south wall, and is covered with stone slabs clamped by iron. There is another between the cenotaphs of Isaac and Rebecca, and this has been completely concealed, the stone flags lying flush over it. The third, the only one still visible, lies just south of the narthex and resembles a marble cup rising out of the floor. It is here, through the perforated lid of the cup, that one can see the light glimmering faintly below. This light however does not shine on the caves, which are close to the south wall of the *haram*, some fifty feet away. The cup leads only to the narrow passageway discovered by Arnulf, and beyond this passageway lies "a round chapel which could hold thirty people." Beyond this chapel lie the two caves. Except for the cenotaph of Isaac none of the existing cenotaphs are near the places where the bones were found.

What happened to the bones? If the prior followed the normal custom of his time, they would have been enclosed in reliquaries and kept in church treasuries and shown to the faithful on high feast days. Small portions of the bones would be given to the Pope and to great princes of the West: so it happened that until recently one could see in a crystal reliquary in the Museum of the Duomo in Florence a sliver of brown bone, no larger and no thicker than a finger-nail, with the accompanying inscription: *S. Abraham.* No doubt many of these fragments were dispersed, but the greater part of the relics remained in Hebron. Sixteen years after the discovery the Arab traveler Abdul Fida came to Hebron and saw the relics displayed. He relates that pious visitors, whether Christian, Arab or Jew, were always permitted to see them.

When Benjamin of Tudela reached Hebron about the year 1163 he found that in addition to six sepulchres built in the church, there were six more underground. The strange proliferation of sepulchres may be explained perhaps by the desire of the monks to reap a profitable harvest. Here is Benjamin of Tudela's account:

> The Christians have erected six sepulchres in this place, which they pretend to be those of Abraham and Sarah, Isaac and Rebecca, Jacob and Leah. The pilgrims are told that these are the sepulchres of the patriarchs, and money is extorted from them. But if any Jew comes, who gives an additional fee to the keeper of the cave, an iron door is opened which dates from the time of their forefathers, who rest in peace, and with a burning candle in his hands the visitor descends into a first cave, which is empty, traverses a second, which is in the same state, and at last reaches a third, which contains six sepulchres—those of Abraham, Isaac and Jacob, and of Sarah, Rebecca, and Leah—one opposite the other.
>
> All these sepulchres bear inscriptions, the letters being engraved. Thus on that of our father Abraham, we read in Hebrew: "This is the tomb of Abraham our father: on him be peace." A lamp burns in the cave and on the sepulchres night and day, and you see here pots filled with the bones of Israelites; for to this day it is the custom of the House of Israel to bring thither the bones of their forefathers, and to leave them there.

Since Benjamin of Tudela is usually remarkably accurate in his observations, we may believe that it was all exactly as he described it. His description of the underground chambers agrees closely with that of the Augustinian canon. The bones were buried again, except for the small portions placed in reliquaries. These bones represented spiritual and financial capital, and the treasure in the cave could always be drawn on in time of need.

The church at Hebron became so powerful and wealthy that inevitably it became a cathedral. In 1167 Gérard d'Auvergne was installed as Archbishop. Twenty years later Archbishop Gérard was in full flight, for Hebron fell to Saladin's army.

Saladin had no time to make major alterations to the sanctuary. The church became a mosque, Saladin himself presenting it with a prayer-niche and the decorated pulpit from Ascalon on which Hussayn's head had once rested. Saladin's nephew Issa (Jesus) took an interest in the mosque and settled on it the rents from two neighboring villages, but it was not until the coming of Baybars, the ferocious Mameluke conqueror from Egypt, that Hebron began to acquire importance in the eyes of the Moslems as a place very nearly as sacred as Mecca. The mosque was reserved for the celebration of the mystery of Abraham, and no non-Moslems were permitted to enter. The soup kitchens traditionally associated with the mosque were ordered out of the *haram* area. There began, slowly at first and then with increasing momentum, the long process by which the shrine became the generator of vast and mysterious forces. Under Baybars the order went out that the caves were to be sealed; only the small cup-shaped orifice near the narthex was to remain open. Great officers of state might be led into the caves. At such times the seals would be broken and the stones rolled back, but this was permitted very rarely. The virtue of the caves was all the greater because they were remote and unseen, and the shadowy shapes could only be guessed at.

Over the small cup-shaped orifice Qalawun, the successor of Baybars, erected a small marble dome, which still remains. Marble slabs were set into the walls, and a marble cenotaph was built in the narthex to represent the presence of Abraham. The remaining cenotaphs appear to have been built during the reign of the Mameluke Sultan Barquq at the end of the fourteenth century. In his reign, too, the bones of Joseph were discovered in Egypt and a seventh cenotaph was accordingly built in a small chamber on the western side of the *haram*. Since that time very few changes have been made.

The years passed, and the power accumulated. From being a shrine the sanctuary at Hebron became a monument, so august and so cherished that no one dared to ask what the monument contained. For centuries no visitor from the West came near it. When Palestine fell to the Ottoman Turks, Jews were permitted to climb up the first seven steps of the long approach to the *haram* and whisper a prayer through a crack in the stone. They were told that the prayer would be heard in the Cave of Machpelah. The same favor was granted to the Christians. For more than six hundred and fifty years no Jew or Christian is known to have entered the *haram*.

On April 7, 1862, the *haram* was opened to a Christian for the first time since Saladin conquered the town.

The unlikely candidate for the honor was the Prince of Wales, the eldest son of Queen Victoria. He was not then the portly, heavily-bearded *bon vivant* who gave his name to an epoch. He was twenty-one, beardless, with curly hair, saucer-blue eyes, an expression of mingled sweetness and arrogance. His father, the Prince Consort, had recently died, and it was thought that a tour of the Near East in the company of his tutors and a small entourage would take his mind off his grief. In Jerusalem he asked the Turkish Governor for permission to enter the *haram*. The Governor was not in fact in a position to grant the permission, and there followed a long and protracted dialogue between the Governor and the Prince, who was assisted by his tutor, Arthur Stanley, a biblical scholar with an iron will. It was Stanley who wanted to enter the *haram*. When the Turkish Governor finally announced that nothing could be done, because it was beyond his power to influence the imam of so holy a shrine, Prince Albert Edward made it clear that he had no intention of remaining any longer in an inhospitable land. The Governor decided to act quickly. The imam was approached, and it was arranged that the prince should be permitted at least to see the cenotaph of Abraham. Soldiers were sent to Hebron to guard the approaches to the sanctuary. Sharpshooters were mounted on roof-tops. Hebron became an armed camp, for it was feared that the Prince would be torn to pieces if his presence became known. In this way, in silence, with the entire population ordered to remain indoors, with guards lining the streets, the Prince entered Hebron, and climbed the long staircase of the *haram*. He had hoped to enter the cave but was shown only the cenotaph of Abraham. Arthur Stanley has left an account of their reception:

> The shrine of Abraham after a momentary hesitation was thrown open. The guardians groaned aloud. But their chief turned to us with the remark: "The Princes of any other nation should have passed over my dead body sooner than enter. But to the eldest son of the Queen of England we are willing to accord even this privilege." He stepped in before us, and offered an ejaculatory prayer to the dead Patriarch: "O Friend of God, forgive this intrusion." We then entered. The chamber is cased in marble. The so-called tomb consists of a coffin-like structure, about six feet high, built up of plastered stone or marble, and hung with three carpets, green embroidered with gold.

They saw nothing more, and a few minutes later they were making their way through the silent streets of Hebron. They had seen only the embroidered carpets on the cenotaph, but they had broken, without knowing it, the centuries-old tradition established by Baybars. Henceforth it would be easier, but not very much easier, for Englishmen to enter the sacred precincts. Viscount Bruce, a close friend of the Prince of Wales, arrived in Hebron in 1866, and was accorded the same privilege. In the eighties Prince George, the son of the Prince of Wales, made the inevitable tour of the Holy Land and he too was permitted to see the cenotaph. Until 1917 no other Englishman is known to have seen it.

In November 1917, when General Allenby was pushing back the Turkish army in Palestine, a young political officer, Colonel Richard Meinertzhagen, found himself in Hebron. The Turks had left only a few hours before, and there were only a few townspeople about. He asked where the notables were, and was told that they had sought refuge in the *haram*. Accordingly he climbed the long stairway, made his way into the mosque, and began to search for the notables. But the mosque and all the outlying buildings were deserted. He knew Arabic well, and shouted that no harm would come to them, but there was no reply. Returning to the *haram*, he saw an opening in the floor and decided to investigate. He was a soldier anxious to establish civil government as quickly as possible in Hebron, and it did not occur to him that this mosque was built over the caves of Machpelah. As he remembered it later, he hurried down the steps cut below the opening in the floor and found himself in a dark cave where the only visible object was a slab of black stone like a tomb, and on each side were two candle-holders carved in a spiral shape. They gleamed, and seemed to be made of metal. The cave was six or seven yards long, and six or seven yards wide. Blackened by smoke and thick with dust, with its solitary tomb and four candle-holders, the cave was thoroughly uninviting, and he was glad to get out. He remembered that there were four stone steps leading down into the cave, but he remembered nothing more. He spent altogether less than five minutes in the *haram*, and it did not occur to him until many years later that he was the first westerner to enter the cave since the time of the Crusaders.

Colonel Meinertzhagen was a highly skilled and resourceful political officer, famous for an exploit which had occurred a few weeks before. He had ridden close to the Turkish lines, giving the impression that he had lost his way, exchanged some shots with the Turks, and then jettisoned a bloodstained rifle and a brief-case which contained a wholly inaccurate set of order papers showing the disposition of Allenby's forces. The Turks fell for the bait, and the colonel had the pleasure of learning that these carefully fabricated papers were regarded with the utmost seriousness by the Turkish high command. The story is told in the official history of the war and even more admiringly by T. E. Lawrence in *Seven Pillars of Wisdom*.

The colonel's account of his brief glimpse of the cave raised as many problems as it solved. The tomb with the four candle-holders was especially puzzling, for nothing quite like this had been encountered in Palestine. It was suggested that he might have seen a Crusader tomb like the one erected for King Baldwin I in the Church of the Holy Sepulchre, which was shaped like a coffin raised on four stone legs. But no, he could remember only the black tomb and the carved candle-holders which seemed to be made of metal.

During the years of the British Mandate over Palestine many scholars visited Hebron. From time to time they were permitted to examine the *haram* closely, to take accurate measurements, and to photograph the interior, but they were never allowed to enter the caves. Father Hugo Vincent of the Order of St. Dominic made a careful examination of the floor-plan, coming to the conclusion that the problem of the exact site of the caves might never be solved.

More than three thousand years have passed since the death of

Abraham, the friend of God, but his mystery endures. In the dawn of history he stands on a lonely eminence, the sun streaming behind him and his face in shadow. We know him for what he was: a wild-bearded tottering old man driven by ferocious passions, and all those passions fed into his love of God. We see him in his tent, and on the rock, and with his wives, wandering across the deserts in search of the Promised Land, and he is always the hard-bitten, untamed Patriarch, with a glory about him. He comes at the beginning of the Old Testament, but he is more living than the kings of Israel and all the prophets, because he alone walks hand in hand with God.

Somewhere under the flag-stones of his shrine at Hebron there may still be the dust of his bones.

THE OLD MAN OF SAMARIA

All I knew about Samaria until I went there was that Jesus walked through it on his way from Galilee to Jerusalem, on one journey healing ten lepers and on another meeting a woman of Sychar at the well and saying many strange things to her about the fields being white already for harvest. I forgot, if I ever knew, that Samaria derives its name from Shemer, who sold it to Omri, King of Israel, for two talents of silver. Then Omri built a city, which was enlarged by his son Ahab, the husband of Jezebel. Ahab built her a house of ivory and erected a temple to Baal, the god of the Phoenicians. Ahab and Jezebel met the fate they so richly deserved, Ahab being killed in battle and Jezebel being thrown from the window by eunuchs. When they looked for her remains, all they could find were her skull, her feet, and the palms of her hands, for the dogs had eaten the rest.

Poor Ahab! Poor Jezebel! And also, more certainly, poor Omri, who was ill-advised to build a city on land bought with silver, and ill-favored in having such a son! Samaria was a place I vaguely associated with tragedy, with blood-feuds, and with cults detestable to the Jews. I had the feeling that Jesus passed through it hurriedly, as a place to be avoided, and never spent a night under a Samaritan roof. Why all this obloquy? Why were so many dogs licking up so much blood?

Certainly the land was fruitful, and the corn grew high, and there were many olive trees at the foot of the soft, rounded mountains. A light mist hung over Mount Gerizim but the sun shone on all the fields below; and there was that shimmering in the air which promises a good harvest.

One day I went to call on the High Priest of the Samaritans, the Most

Reverend Nugi Khadiz Kahen. He looked like an aged eagle, his face deeply lined, black veins throbbing at his temples, his hooked nose and thin lips giving him an appearance of subdued ferocity. There was much gentleness in him, and he liked to make slow, sweeping gestures with his frail and bony hands. He wore a scarlet cloth round his black hat as a badge or crown of authority. He told me he was the 146th in direct line of descent from Aaron, and permitted himself a short pause to allow this news to sink in. "From Aaron," he repeated, and a small smile of satisfaction lit up the ancient face.

Soon the satisfaction gave place to anger as he described the oppressions inflicted on the Samaritans throughout the centuries. They had committed no crimes, they had held fast to the true beliefs and preserved the holy traditions, and yet they had suffered abominably from their neighbors. Every man's hand was against them. The Jews especially oppressed them, and this was because the Jews had developed their own interpretation of the scriptures. Moses was the only true Prophet of God, and only the Pentateuch—the first five books of the Old Testament—was divinely inspired. Joshua constructed the first Tabernacle on Mount Gerizim, the holy mountain, and there was no other holy mountain. Mount Moriah in Jerusalem was unholy, had not been sanctioned by God, and Solomon's temple, and all the rites that took place in it, were abominations. The truth had been given only to Samaritans who alone were chosen by God.

"But the world does not see or understand this," the high priest explained. "The world is blind! Especially the world of the Jews!"

He spoke with great vehemence, his thin lips curling in derision. He quivered with anger as he spoke of the abominations committed in the name of Moses.

I asked him how many Samaritans survived, expecting him to say there were many thousands, enough to populate a few towns in Samaria. He said there were three hundred and eighty-eight. About seventy of them were priests who lived on the charity of the rest, who were mostly poor. The tragedy was that they were often too poor to marry, with the result that the race was dying out.

"We cannot die," he insisted, "because we are God's chosen ones. Even though we are very few, we must do God's work. You must help us! Everyone must help us!"

The schism had taken place so long ago that no one could remember exactly how it happened. Perhaps it can be traced back to 720 B.C. when Samaria was the capital of Israel and the Assyrian armies came down like the wolf on the fold; and thousands were slaughtered, thousands more went into Babylonian exile, and the few left behind in Samaria regarded themselves as the chosen ones, the elect of God, the true inheritors. They had been saved from exile, and became proud and erected their own temple on the heights of Mount Gerizim. But the schism between the Samaritans and the Jews was now complete, and the enmity long lasting. In 109 B.C. John Hyrcanus, the Jewish High Priest, destroyed Samaria and razed the Samaritan temple to the ground. Yet the Samaritans survived; they had a lust for survival. They survived the Roman occupation by working with the Romans against the Jews, and under Hadrian they were permitted to build their temple again. In A.D. 530 in the reign of the Byzantine emperor Justinian they revolted, burned the Christian churches and destroyed the monasteries. Justinian was pitiless. The Byzantine army marched into Samaria and few Samaritans survived the ordeal. Within a hundred years all Palestine was conquered by the Moslems. Then for many centuries very little was heard from the Samaritans.

As a special privilege—although I suspect it was a privilege accorded to all his well-meaning visitors—the High Priest offered to show me the earliest known copy of the Pentateuch. It was written in Phoenician characters within thirty years of the Hebrew occupation of Palestine, which would place it about 1130 B.C. It lay in an ornate silver box, and was evidently very old and frail, the parchment crackling as it was unrolled. It was beyond belief that the scroll was as old as Moses. There was another old parchment with a drawing showing the original arrangement of the objects in the Ark of the Covenant: the cherubim, the mercy seat, the seven-branched candlestick, the basins and ewers, and the cherubim were wide-winged birds hovering serenely over the mercy seat.

With a young Samaritan we drove up the winding path which leads close to the summit of Mount Gerizim. A gusting wind was blowing, and the yellow corn flowers waved wildly. The young Samaritan was tall, thin-boned, thickly bearded, with dark heavily lidded eyes as intense as those of the High Priest. At the very top of the mountain there were a few broken marble columns, all that was left of the ancient Samaritan temple. Here, according to Samaritan practice, they hold Passover every year. Robed in white, eating only unleavened bread, they chant and clap hands for seven days and nights.

"You must understand you are walking on holy ground," the young Samaritan was saying. "Here, on this mountain, Abraham prepared to sacrifice Isaac, and here Moses received the tablets of the law, and here Jacob was buried, and here, and only here, the Shekinah, the divine light, touches the earth. You see, to us, and to us alone, there has been given the truth!"

All I know is that it was splendid up there, with the grasses and the sunflowers blowing. To the west the clouds were piling up for a blood-red sunset, and soon there were streamers of scarlet and gold flowing down on the holy mountain.

THE PLACE OF TREMBLING

"If they build any more monasteries and basilicas, poor Nazareth will perish under their weight," the young priest was saying. "I don't believe buildings bring us closer to God. I believe we have to build in our own hearts."

He was a French priest with a stubble beard and dark pouches under his eyes. He had spent the night at the bedside of an Arab Christian who died shortly before dawn; now worn out, exhausted by the long vigil, with that look of helplessness and despair which is inevitable after such a night, he was having breakfast in a cheap restaurant near the bus station. Blue eyes gazed out of the drawn face; high cheekbones; a stubborn, bony chin; an elegance of manner which betrayed his origins in the south of France. At the moment he dipped his bread in the coffee, there came another dynamite explosion from the top of the hill where they were building the new basilica of the Annunciation. His eyebrows rose, his hand trembled, and he gave a little half-apologetic smile.

"We are building," he went on, "but to build the City of God—that is something else. Sometimes I think they will never be satisfied until they have crowned with a huge basilica every place where Jesus walked. It surprises me that they have not built another vast basilica at Cana, and at the place of his baptism, and in the middle of the Sea of Galilee. A floating cathedral! Yes, you can go on from there! What does a building signify except that a man can put two stones together? There is a bigger cathedral in the human heart than any made by human hands. Think of the beginnings! A few men walking and preaching, and the Son of Man had nowhere to rest his head. Wanderers floating with the wind! We drive a stake in the earth and put a sign over it, and say: "Here he was!" The truth is we don't know where he was, and it doesn't matter! What matters is that he was, and is! Let them think no more about building basilicas!"

It was not unusual to find priests in the Holy Land who deplored the building of new churches. There were even some who deplored the streams of pilgrims to the holy shrines, saying, as men said in the Middle Ages, that you could have Jerusalem in your heart even if you lived in some remote village of northern France and men's souls are not saved by pilgrimage.

It was that hour of the morning when Nazareth is bustling with activity, the sunlight pouring down on the narrow streets, the Arabs in their white gowns and white *keffiyas* hurrying about their business as though time was running out, street hawkers shouting, the shopkeepers standing eagerly at the doors of the terrible little shops where they sold souvenirs and cheap cloth, and children running off to school. Soon the town would grow quieter and by midday you would find scarcely anyone except the tourists wandering through the streets.

The priest was bone-tired, but the long and terrible night had left him in no mood to sleep, and so we walked together to the Virgin's Well, which is enclosed in a Greek Orthodox church. There in the cool bubbling waters of the well he bathed his face, and it must have been then or a little later that I told him about the Tremore, the Place of Trembling, high up on the scrub-covered hill facing us. I had been impressed by the beauty and simplicity of this small church set in a saddle of the hill and standing against the skyline. At the far end of the hill there was a wonderful view of the plains from the edge of a precipice. From very early times this precipice had been identified with the brow of the hill, mentioned in *Luke*, from which some people of Nazareth had hoped to cast Jesus down headlong, "but he passing through the midst of them went his way." The Tremore was the place where Mary had stood transfixed in fear and trembling, as the mob gathered around Jesus and threatened to kill him.

The priest had never seen this church nor had he ever stood on the edge of the precipice, and so we walked up some steep paths beside a quarry, talking about Nazareth and the priestly life and all the problems of living in a Christian Arab community. The weariness was visibly leaving him.

He said: "When St. Louis came to Nazareth, he prayed so devoutly in his hair-shirt that everyone around him was afraid for his life. He prayed with so much devotion, for so long, and taking so little food, that he nearly died. He had come to conquer the Holy Land but the Holy Land conquered him, and he stayed too long for his own good."

"Then one shouldn't fall in love with the Holy Land?"

"It is better not to fall in love with anyone except God," the priest said, and already the Tremore, the small church on the saddle of the hill, was coming in view.

I had fallen in love with the Tremore a long time ago during my first visit to the Holy Land. I imagined it was built by the Crusaders because the proportions were so pure, so august, and so simple; it represented Romanesque art in its ultimate refinement. So I thought until one day I learned that it was built much more recently by a Russian baroness in memory of her husband, a high official killed by terrorists during the closing years of the last century. Nevertheless the architect had based the small church on Romanesque models and achieved a magnificent building with springing columns over a porch and a stairway over a crypt, and all of it with wonderful proportions. I was glad the priest admired it. I had already visited it four or five times, every time I passed through Nazareth, and I was looking forward to seeing it again from a carefully chosen vantage point a little to one side, about thirty feet away. Already it stood proudly on the skyline, gleaming white against the sky, looking at this distance more like a palace with a covered portico than a church.

Just at this moment four Arab boys in long white skirts emerged from behind the church. They were shouting and gesticulating, waving their arms, but not invitingly. There was something menacing in the way they came down the mountain toward us. They were not shouting so much as screaming and cursing. The priest said: "They are telling us to get off their mountain."

"It is not their mountain!"

"They are telling us to go away, and they mean business!"

We went on walking toward them out of habit, scarcely believing we were being ordered off by Arab boys who looked too small to create any mischief. We thought we would talk to them, perhaps give them some *baksheesh,* and then go on our way unmolested. Suddenly we heard a crack, as a stone hit a branch above our heads. They were aiming at us with catapults. Stones kept falling all around us, or we heard them whistling past our ears, or they rattled against the leaves above our heads. The four boys were joined by two more, so that there seemed to be a small army of them coming down the hill. One stone hit me in the shoulder and left a bruise that lasted a week. "They mean business!" the priest said, and a moment later we were racing down the mountain, confused and angry. Sometimes we looked back to see the boys running after us, pausing to aim with their catapults, and then running again, advancing, running, gaining on us, until by good fortune we found a path near the quarry that brought us close to the main road leading into Nazareth.

"I saw an Arab die early this morning, and the last thing that would ever have occurred to me was that a bunch of Arab boys would be trying to kill us on the Mount of the Precipitation an hour later," the priest was saying. "The next time I go and see the Tremore I'll make sure to take some Arab boys with me."

He laughed grimly. A moment later he was saying: "Can any good thing come out of Nazareth? Of course good things come out of Nazareth, but the bad endures. Sometimes it puzzles me. The boys wanted the whole mountain for themselves, but for how long can they keep a mountain? Possess nothing, and you have everything!"

The bus for Tiberias and the Sea of Galilee was waiting at the bus station. I climbed into the creaking, oily bus, filled with Arabs and Druzes. For a few moments the priest stood by the window.

"Thank you for taking me to the Tremore," he said, and there was the faintest gleam of malice in his tired eyes.

Then he walked away with long strides in the direction of the great basilica which threatens to crush Nazareth with its weight.

THE SEA OF GALILEE

In those days I was always coming or going to the Sea of Galilee. I remember restless days in Beersheba and Jerusalem when I found myself dreaming of the lake and wondering why I ever left it. The colors and shape of the lake, and all its many moods, possess a compelling beauty, and one returns to it again and again in the same way that one returns to a work of art. I was always walking round it, climbing the hills to see it better, or fishing in it, or taking a motorboat out in it, or simply gazing at it from the best vantage point of all, which is the Mount of the Beatitudes, high up, so that the entire lake comes into view with all its inlets and promontories. The Hebrews called it Kinnereth, meaning "the harp," but it is not really harp-shaped. It is much closer to the shape of the human heart.

I can remember no day when the lake was not entirely pleasing. It was very feminine, diaphanous, trembling. It changed color every twenty minutes, and moved easily and carelessly from an intensely deep blue to a soft emerald to violet, but mostly it was a kind of emerald-blue. It changes color according to the wind or the clouds or the humidity of the air, and this constant change of color gives it a curious evanescence, so that you have the feeling that it exists on the very edge of things and at any moment will vanish into nothingness. Perhaps because the lake is below sea level colors seem to be brighter and voices louder, and the ordinary world is far away. Jerusalem is of the earth earthy, all stone and rock, hard enough to test the spirits of the sternest prophets, and the lake is all grace and beauty, a place for dreams and visions.

It was always a little dangerous to go out on the lake, because Syrian guns were mounted on the Golan Heights. From time to time a Syrian gunner would let loose a few rounds of ammunition to relieve the monotony of his life on the heights. They were good marksmen, had killed many people, and seemed determined to go on killing. We were therefore advised whenever we took out the motorboats not to go too far across the lake. When we asked: "How far is far?" they answered: "Two or three hundred feet from the shore. If you go any farther, they will be unable to resist the temptation of taking some pot shots at you." But there was also the temptation to take the motorboat far out on the lake, which resembled a mirage, wholly unreal, and therefore without any hint of danger. The lake was another sky, and to go out on it was to float unfettered in the heavens.

Of course there were mysteries in the lake. On the lake and on its shores mysterious things had happened which profoundly affected the course of history. In the shimmer and dazzle of this unearthly light Jesus announced the beatitudes, cured the sick, gave sight to the blind, raised the dead, fed the five thousand, and walked on the lake during a storm. At Cana, near the lake, he performed the first miracle, and at Mount Tabor, overlooking the lake, he was transfigured. At Nazareth, less than a day's journey from the lake, he grew to manhood, and on the shores of the lake he found the fishermen who became his disciples.

We do not have to wonder what brought him to the lake; it was his natural home and appointed rest, the place he continually returned to, where he was known to nearly everyone and could find shelter and a hiding place with the greatest of ease. Although we know very little for certain about him, we know that he was a sojourner by the lakeside. He belonged to that trembling and ever-changing light, to colors that melted into one another, to a landscape as close to paradise as anything one can imagine.

Here Jesus walked in dreams and saw visions, and these dreams and visions were colored by the lake light, by the glint of the yellow rocks, the silken waters, the heavens that opened out to reveal immense blue towers and palaces. It is a landscape enclosed, full of imaginings, the landscape of fairy tales and also of a grave tenderness, where everything is possible —even the Kingdom of Heaven. The special quality of the lake, its trembling light and the quivering in the air, can scarcely be put into words at all; the closest we come to it is perhaps in the early English devotional song "I sing of a maiden":

He cam also stille
Ther his moder was,
As dew in Aprille
That fallith on the gras.

He cam also stille
To his moderes bowr,
As dew in Aprille
That fallith on the flowr.

He cam also stille
There his moder lay,
As dew in Aprille
That fallith on the spray.

In Galilee the air is filled with the running of the dew, everything sparkles, the earth is caught up in a hush of expectancy, and it would not be in the least surprising to see a man walking across the lake. At every turning of the lakeside road you half expect to see an angel, a King riding on a painted elephant, or Isaiah. If the Queen of Galilee herself came walking along the road, you would salute her gravely and pass on. Cecil Sharp, wandering through the mountainous wasteland of Southern Appalachia in 1917, heard from an old settler an old English carol, which appears in many versions but none quite so magnificent as the version discovered in America:

Joseph was a young man,
A young man was he.
He courted Virgin Mary,
The Queen of Galilee.

As Joseph and Mary
Were walking one day,
Here is apples and cherries
Enough to behold.

Then Mary spoke to Joseph
So neat and so mild:
Joseph, gather me some cherries,
For I am with child.

Then Joseph flew in angry,
In angry he flew;
Let the father of the baby
Gather cherries for you.

Lord Jesus spoke a few words,
All down unto them,
Bow low down, low down, cherry tree,
Let the mother have some.

The cherry tree bowed low down,
Low down to the ground,
And Mary gathered cherries
While Joseph stood around.

Then Joseph took Mary
All on his right knee.
He cried: O Lord have mercy
For what have I done.

And Joseph took Mary
All on his left knee.
Pray tell me little baby
When will your birthday be?

On the fifth day of January
My birthday will be,
When the stars and the elements
Doth tremble with fear.

The song, of course, is a fairy tale full of implausible events made plausible by the heat of the poet's imagination. We believe while we listen; afterward there are second thoughts. We wonder why the Queen of Galilee should be sitting now on Joseph's right knee, now on his left knee, and why should her birthday fill the stars and the elements with fear? We tell ourselves that her birthday is not her birthday, but the day on which she gives birth, and in fact Christmas was often celebrated early in January. But none of these explanations really help us to understand the poem, which is pure magic. Galilee is feminine, and Jerusalem is harshly masculine, and both are magical. But the magic of Galilee belongs to women and children, and is all tenderness, while the magic of Jerusalem is hammered out of power and authority, the gaunt father figure who ultimately becomes the world emperor, the law-giver, the supreme judge. Galilee and Jerusalem are sheer antipodes, for one is ruled by the Queen and the other by the King. It is as though they were two universes obeying completely different physical laws, and it would seem that there was almost no communication between them. Yet, as we know, the communication was made in the journey that brought Jesus from the lake to the Cross.

By the lake all things seem possible, all questions are answered, all doubts are set at rest. In the early morning when a light mist touches the lake, strange shadows appear in it, and there are a few moments when the lake appears to be without shape or substance, to be boiling over like milk. Then quite suddenly the mist is burned away, leaving a pool of silvery blue that shoots across the lake with enormous speed and strikes against the yellow shores. For the rest of the day the lake will wear that deep burnished golden blue, the blue that is Mary's color, the royal blue of the Queen of Galilee.

LEBANON

THE FACES OF BEYROUT

I flew from Amman to Beyrout on a day when the clouds lay like golden fleece below, while high above us, like remnants of an ancient golden age blown sky high, were other clouds of darker gold hammered into the shape of wings with torn and ragged feathers; and so between the golden fleece below and the fiery feathers above we flew out of the sandy deserts toward the Mediterranean. It was evening when we landed at Beyrout. The feathers and the fleece had vanished; there was only a grey crepuscular sky, dark and ominous, streaked with black clouds that were once hammered gold. The airport was a place of menace. The airplane landed half a mile from the customs house; we were ordered to march across the tarmac; the customs inspection was interminable; luggage was lost; it was late at night before we reached our hotels.

The first impression was bad, the second was worse, and the third made up for all that went before. I hated Beyrout the next morning. After the silence of the desert the deafening noise of the place seemed meaningless and incomprehensible. It was a city of jackhammers and power drills, of people shouting and arguing, of thousands of automobiles racing through the streets as purposelessly as frightened ants when an anthill is overturned. The color of the sky was theatrical, the smell of gasoline fumes hung heavy in the air, and there was the acid reek of luxury. Jerusalem and Amman were both humble places. Beyrout flaunted its wealth and paraded its softness, inviting the visitor to drown in its warmth and its fat. A soft sea bathed the city, and we were very far from the naked rocks of the desert.

In the following days I tried to come to terms with Beyrout. I walked the streets determinedly, looking at houses and shops, and coming to no conclusions except that the houses were wonderfully ill-designed and the shops were full of too many luxuries which even the Beyroutians could scarcely afford. There was a museum that half-heartedly attempted to show the glories of ancient Lebanon. There were arrowheads, stone obelisks dating from 5000 B.C., skeletons of neolithic men buried in four-foot, red-clay jars. Above all, in the gloomy basement lay the huge sarcophagi of Phoenician kings, including the sarcophagus of Ahiram, King of Byblos, who reigned about 1200 B.C. The sarcophagus is an impressively massive work, powerful and ungainly, yet with a sense of controlled, brutal magnificence. We see the tribute bearers marching along the sides of the sarcophagus to offer tribute to the king on his lion throne, while his wives in strange flounced dresses raise their arms in lamentation and beat their breasts. On the lid of the sarcophagus is an inscription giving the king's titles in a calligraphy which is clearly the ancestor of our alphabet. Then there are rooms full of jewelry and others full of Roman mosaics, including a vivid Bacchus with a commanding presence and a fiery glance. On a sarcophagus of the third century B.C. the sculptor has carved a ship with full sails which looks sturdy enough to ride through Mediterranean storms. The ship reminds you that the Phoenicians from Byblos, Tyre and Sidon were the first deep-sea navigators and the first empire builders to establish colonies overseas: they conquered the Aegean islands, Cyprus, Malta, large areas of North Africa and eastern Spain, and their ships sailed out into the Atlantic to trade with Brittany and to bargain with tin-miners in Cornwall. They fought the Romans almost to a standstill and were within an inch of becoming the rulers of the Mediterranean world. Now Byblos, Tyre and Sidon, once great imperial ports, are little more than villages hugging the seacoast. The empire perished, but it left to the Western world one imperishable legacy—the alphabet.

"The strength of the Egyptians is to sit still," wrote Ralph Waldo Emerson. It appeared that the strength of the Beyroutians was to run about at a mad pace. The problem was to discover what they were running after. I never learned what made them so frantically active, so noisy, so improbably filled with a wild gaiety. I took to studying their faces and came to some conclusions which surprised me, though they are perhaps obvious to students of Lebanon. Lebanon is the melting pot. Greeks,

Egyptians, Jews, Arabs, Syrians, Bedouin from the Hedjaz and Hadh-ramaut, oil princes from Kuwait and Oman, Iraqis and Turks are gradually fusing together a new race representing not the Levant only but every other race included within the wide trade-circle that has its center in Beyrout. The process, of course, has been going on for a long time, but the pace is now rapidly increasing. The melting pot is being stirred, and through the steam it is possible to discern new faces compounded out of all the races of the Levant.

In Lebanon you scarcely ever see a face that is not pleasing. Eyes are large and lustrous. They have high cheekbones, full lips, strong chins, and walk nimbly. Occasionally you come upon flaxen-haired Arab boys with blue eyes who must be descended in direct line from the Crusaders. They are a people who live dangerously, and this too influences their features, giving them a sharpness and keenness they would not otherwise possess. Crowded into their narrow coastline, they have the gaiety of a people living perpetually on the edge of an abyss. Instead of being dismayed by danger, they seem to exult in it. "We survive," one of them told me, "by a series of miracles." Happy are those who enjoy so many miracles!

BAALBEK

From Beyrout the road climbs merrily up the Lebanon mountains, past the umbrella pines and the white palaces of Arab sheikhs, past the night clubs which look sad and haunted during the day but will be festooned with a blaze of lights during the evening, past red-roofed villages set among orchards and pink villas perched on cliffs, and the journey is oddly unreal, as though you were traveling through a landscape labeled: *The Slopes of Luxury.* For Beyrout is very rich and the steep mountainside flaunts its riches with a gay abandonment.

As you drive up that winding road, the world seems to fall away. You find yourself hovering in mid-air between the clouds and the sea in a state of languorous euphoria and dizziness appropriate to the very rich or to those who are traveling very fast. And also there was a sense of danger and menace, but this came chiefly from the driver I hired at the Phoenicia Hotel. He had a rough, heavy face, small glinting eyes, an expansive manner, and the look of a man who is not averse to a little double-dealing. It was a mistake to have hired him, and by the time we were beginning to climb the mountain I knew I was in trouble. I also knew it was too late to do anything about it.

There came a time when I thought he was the most menacing person I had ever encountered, for he could scarcely open his mouth without hinting at the fate reserved for me. He explained that there was very little traffic on the road, there had been many murders, and for this reason he always carried a gun in a shoulder holster. He boasted wildly, told lies outrageously, and was a prey to all the Levantine follies. He announced that he had a loving wife, six children and four mistresses, owned several businesses, many of them exceedingly profitable, and as for the fare he had originally charged, that, *monsieur,* was still subject to discussion "as between friends" and he proposed to return to the subject at a later and more suitable time. He asked me how much money I was carrying, and seemed surprised by the answer. By this time I had decided to pay him off when we reached Baalbek, for it was obviously absurd to travel with a man who was dangerously psychopathic. Once I asked him why, if he was so wealthy and so powerful, he chose to make a living as a taxi-driver. He thought about this for some time and then allowed that it was a good way of making money particularly when the passengers are "good comrades." Meanwhile he continued to drive at seventy miles an hour round hairpin bends.

The air of menace subsided a little when we reached the Bekaa, the vast plain between the Lebanon and Antilebanon mountains. Suddenly the earth was red, there were cherry orchards, forests of apple trees, vineyards. There was luxury in Beyrout; here there was luxuriance. The enclosing arms of the two mountain ranges forced water into the valley, with the result that every leaf and every blade of grass was fat. Although there was luxuriance, the peasants looked poor and drab, unsmiling, and it appeared that the wealth of the valley poured into the pockets of the absentee landowners. It was real wealth, a richer earth than I had seen anywhere else in the Middle East, and the air was scented. Far away we could see the snow on the Antilebanon mountains.

By this time I had grown so accustomed to deserts that the sight of a flowering plain came almost as an impertinence. I thought of the Israelis cultivating their fields so carefully and cautiously, the water-sprinklers fuming into rainbows, and how difficult it was except in Galilee to make anything grow. Here it was all so easy, so preposterously easy. Even the driver was smiling at this plain which was so wide, so deep, and so blessed with green things. The air smelled of all the fats of the earth.

Suddenly we were in Baalbek with the six enormous columns of the Temple of Jupiter riding high over the small red-roofed town. The columns were the color of frozen honey, majestic, imperial, splendid in their proportions. There was movement in them; they sprang up urgently; they commanded the valley; they possessed a soaring elegance and luxuriance, like everything that grew in the Bekaa. It was as though they were the natural product of that immensely fertile valley: they were tight sheaves of wheat parading their fruitfulness to the sky. These columns have a hypnotic effect, and wherever you turn they seem to be there.

The puzzling thing about the great complex of temples at Baalbek is that no one knows for certain who built them, or when they were built, or what gods they celebrated, or why so often and so unexpectedly the accepted canons of Roman architecture were subtly altered. No dedicatory inscriptions have been found, nor are there any free-standing statues of the gods who were worshiped, nor are there any surviving historical records, nor are there any traditions. The Byzantine historian John Malala of Antioch, writing in the early sixth century, said that Antoninus Pius, the successor of Hadrian, "built a great temple of the sun at Heliopolis near Libanus in Phoenicia, which was one of the wonders of the world." John Malala is not an especially reputable historian, and it is very unlikely that Antoninus Pius, always cautious and sober-minded, would have countenanced such a dazzling and wildly exuberant project. Historians are now inclined to believe that the temples in their final form were erected at the orders of Septimus Severus and his murderous son Antoninus Caracalla, who belonged to the short-lived Syrian dynasty of Roman emperors. The fact that no dedicatory inscriptions have been found can be easily explained. Baalbek fell to the Christians and then to the Moslems, and both Christians and Moslems were delighted to smash the pagan gods and obliterate all inscriptions, and they might have gone on to destroy the temples altogether if it had been humanly possible. They could not destroy the temples completely because never before or since have men worked with such massive stones. In a neighboring quarry you can see a hewn stone intended for the temple which measures sixty-nine by sixteen by fourteen feet and weighs a thousand tons.

In the study of history we usually find that men make their most grandiose monuments during the period when the nation is on the verge of decline. Edward Gibbon thought the decline of the Roman empire began with the reign of Septimus Severus. As you wander among the ruins of Baalbek, you are made aware of a giant striving, of massive achievement, of a limit beyond which it was not possible to go. Megalomania has achieved its goal.

Nevertheless those six surviving columns are wonderfully impressive.

Temple of Jupiter at Baalbek

Temple of Bacchus at Baalbek

Sarcophagus of Ahiram, King of Byblos, with earliest known alphabetical writing above

Phoenician ship relief on third century B.C. sarcophagus, Beyrout Museum

Roman mosaic of Bacchus from Byblos, Beyrout Museum

Byblos. Twelfth-century Crusader
castle with Roman colonnade in
background

Neolithic burial egg from Byblos

They stand on their high platform like a superb work of art, beautiful in themselves and in their coloring; and one would not wish to have more, and less than five would be too few. Robert Wood, traveling in Lebanon in 1749, found nine columns still standing and drew a picture showing them in an immaculate line like giant soldiers on parade. Nine are too many. They clutter the view. If there were twenty it would be bearable, for then we would be able to visualize the whole temple. The six honey-colored columns, which are eighty-one feet high, appear to have very little to do with a temple. They are gloriously *there.*

THE GOLDSMITH

He was a small man with a lean face and a scar reaching from his ear to his chin. It was a particularly livid scar, and you had the impression that he must have received the knife-wound only a few days ago. Sometimes, as he talked, he would touch the scar delicately and reflectively, as though it was the source of many memories. He spoke French with a heavy Lebanese singsong, and was continually moving his hands, not gesticulating with a desire to emphasize, but caressingly, with a desire to soften and humanize the words he spoke so gravely, as though the fate of the world hung on them. His small shop looked out on the small ruined Temple of Venus, and beyond this you could see the immense honey-colored columns of the Syrian Jupiter.

I had bought some damask cloth in the center of Baalbek, and the old man who owned the shop had spoken of a nephew or a cousin who owned this small goldsmith's shop. It appeared that this shop had a long history and was notable for the quality of the workmanship and in addition the prices were superlatively cheap. "I will accompany you myself," said the seller of damask cloth, and was as good as his word. And so we went off in a taxi to the goldsmith's shop and the seller of damask cloth made the suitable introductions. Everything was done on the level of colloquies between plenipotentiaries. Gold figurines, gold bracelets and anklets, gold necklaces gleamed in the windows. Coffee was served, and the plenipotentiaries murmured politely to one another. I heard myself introduced as a man who has studied deeply in the history of Lebanon, was a friend of the country, and therefore deserved to be shown the treasures hidden from the less deserving. All this, of course, was the preliminary to the preliminaries. We sat over coffee discussing the state of the world which, as usual, was in a deplorable condition. The man with the scar thought it would get worse while believing that Lebanon would grow richer. Had I observed the new palaces built by the Arab sheikhs on the mountains above Beyrout? It appeared that Lebanon would survive, while the world crumbled.

I was fascinated by the Arab circumlocutions, the easy filigree of conversation. It occurred to me that I had no business at all in the goldsmith's shop and that I would be able to spend my time better wandering again through the palace of Bacchus and climbing the foothills of the Temple of the Syrian Jupiter. What was I doing there in a room where every glass case contained treasure? The Lebanese singsong continued unabated, as effortless as dreams. The seller of damask cloth was describing the recent history of Lebanon, which seemed to be curiously uneventful in comparison with the history of its neighbors. Suddenly the calm was broken as a voice said: "Have you shown him your best treasures, Sidi?" A long pause, another gulp of coffee. "Remember, the very best, Sidi. You know he is very interested in coins." There was a confused movement in the back of the shop. The man with the scar was rummaging in the back of the shop, taking his time, as though he were selecting among a hundred trays of coins the one which would most surely appeal to me, or perhaps he was searching for the one supreme coin, the single masterpiece larger and more beautiful than any coin I had ever seen. Finally he emerged from the darkness with a three-tiered tray and on the top tier there were perhaps twenty coins embedded in white cotton all glinting in the full sunlight pouring through the windows. There were coins of Alexander the Great and of his successors, each coin nestling on its fluffy pillow. On the second tier there were Byzantine coins, and on the third Arabic coins. As the three tiers opened up, it was possible to see a King's ransom in gold.

As it happened, I was not particularly interested in gold coins. It was much more rewarding, and more amusing, to watch the Lebanese goldsmith and his uncle assuming, discarding and then assuming again the strange conspiratorial air which, to all appearances, had become an essential element in their lives. Quick glances, superb gestures, fluttering of silk gowns, hands suddenly shooting out of embroidered sleeves, and once the old man pulled back his sleeve and rolled it up a little to reveal the crimson silk lining and to show beyond any doubt that his sleeves were not hiding any gold coins.

At the sight of the gold the old man quivered with excitement and pleasure. His lips were pursed, his eyes ran over them like a man reading a beloved and familiar text, and sometimes he made curious muttering noises. I could hear their breathing; it was the calm breathing of people who were at peace with themselves and immune from the temptations of this world.

"Have you ever seen anything like this?" the old man was saying. "Such mint condition. *Cher monsieur,* they are all yours."

I was sufficiently familiar with the marketplaces of the East to know that what is yours is always mine, and that however long the process of bargaining there comes a time when for all practical purposes the bargaining is merely a dance around a fixed point. The dance had not yet begun. Now we were immersed in the process of seduction which is conducted with grace and a certain compassion for the victim.

"Choose, my dear friend," the old man went on. "Take them in your hands. Examine them closely with this magnifying glass. We are not salesmen. We are vendors of pure delight. We shall quote a special price for you. It is our prayer that you will carry away with you the fondest memories of this little shop in Baalbek."

I said something about a gold stater of Alexander looking so clean and fresh that it might have been made yesterday, and a frown crossed the old man's lined and leathery face. His nephew whispered something in his ear and went off in search of another tray; this time it was Roman coins, and they seemed, if possible, even more mint-fresh, more beautiful, and more commanding. The bold faces of the Roman emperors were stamped out with brilliant precision. A heavily jowled but still youthful Nero was astonishingly lifelike; the thin, pinched face of Tiberius looked even more menacing in gold. It was difficult to choose among them because each coin seemed to be about as perfect as it was possible for a coin to be. The Byzantine coins were perhaps less satisfying because no attempt had been made to reproduce the features of the emperors; there was merely a kind of rapid sketch, without depth, and the Arabic coins, of course, showed no portraits of the Caliphs, only interlaced Arabic inscriptions. Yet all of them were appealing and wonderfully made.

"How do you like them?" the old man crooned, as he filled my coffee-cup.

"It's impossible to choose between them because they are all magnificent."

"I told you so," the old man said to his nephew. "He knows everything that is to be known about coins." And then turning to me: "You will find nothing like them anywhere else! Of course every dealer has a few good coins, but you will never find a collection like this! Never! Tell me a single shop in Beyrout which has coins like this! You will not find one, and why? Because the coins are found here in Baalbek, which is exactly where you would expect to find them. The Greeks, the Romans, the Byzantines and Arabs all ruled here, this was their capital, and that is why so much gold has been found. You must understand that Baalbek is the source. In each case my nephew will quote a special price, because you are my friend. You will agree that our prices are very reasonable."

When he began to recite the prices, I was not convinced that they were reasonable. I thought they were outrageous, and said he was stretching friendship too far to expect me to pay five times what they were worth. This was a signal for the old man to huddle with his nephew with much gesturing and demonstrating with fingers. They whispered nervously together, and then the old man said: "Sidi agrees with me to cut ten percent off the prices quoted to you. This is done as a mark of friendship to you. We know you will come back once you have bought these coins."

"I think you should cut off at least fifty percent."

"You are joking with us?"

"Not in the least."

"We would be ruined, my dear friend, if we sold them so cheaply. It is true we are not merchants, but we have to pay our expenses. We give good prices to the peasants who find these coins for us, we have terrible overhead expenses, and we have to pay taxes. You would blush with shame if you knew how much we pay for taxes! You understand, we would like to give them to you—they are yours—we are your slaves—we ask only a fair price. The Nero you admire so much, it is a gift at a hundred dollars, truly it is a gift! And the Tiberius?" He turned to his nephew and said: "He likes the Tiberius, too. You see, he really understands about coins!

Give him a special price for the Tiberius! Dear Sidi, just this once favor me with your kindness! Let him have the Tiberius for seventy-five dollars!"

The seduction was taking place with alarming ease. I was dazzled by the beauty of the coins, the flash of gold, the light pouring through the window, the fumes of coffee, the elaborate gestures, the soft intriguing voices, the murmur of silk. They hovered over me like gentle-faced vultures, while I held up the coins and examined them under a magnifying glass. Nero and Tiberius could be resisted as being too monumental and too expensive. A gold coin of Alexander the Great, an idealized portrait ordered by Lysimachus not long after Alexander's death, proved irresistible. It was scarcely larger than a fingernail, but every detail was brilliantly clear; the wide-open eyes, the expression of petulant majesty, the curving ram's horn, and even the delicate waving fillets were perfectly cut. The winds of summer were blowing through his hair. Nor could I resist a coin of Valentinian I, wearing the diadem, who was almost as handsome as Alexander. He was one of the few Roman emperors who defended the people against officials, fought the Huns to a standstill, marched across Illyria, Africa and England, built hospitals for the Roman poor, and wore with some grace the title "Restitutor Respublicae." He had a terrible temper and died of an attack of apoplexy while talking to the Illyrian ambassador. The third coin showed the Byzantine Emperor Theophilus on one side and on the other his father Michael II the Stammerer and his son Michael III the Drunkard. They were three perfectly useless emperors, and Michael III was stabbed to death by his close friend Basil, who thereupon founded the longest lasting Byzantine dynasty. I had never seen three generations of emperors on a single coin, nor had I ever possessed a Byzantine coin. One Greek, one Roman, one Byzantine. It was a good beginning. They could be bought at a price I could afford, and I was grateful for the hours spent poring over the coins.

"Perhaps we could tempt him by offering an even better price for the Tiberius," the old man was saying, but it was too late. The vision of being the possessor of a whole treasure chest of ancient coins was fading. Baalbek with its strange soaring columns was glowing in the evening light as I walked out of the goldsmith's shop.

Some weeks later, in New York, I showed the three coins to a friend who knew more about coins than I shall ever know. He examined them carefully.

"All fakes, of course," he said. "Where did you get them? In Lebanon?"

BYBLOS

One day I came to the end of the journey in the world's oldest town, near a red river and among tombs shaped like giant eggs. Long before the Pharaohs, long before Greece and Rome, there was a settlement at Byblos with walls and tombs and temples sacred to the gods of the Phoenicians. These people were traders almost before trading began; and this seaport, though only a few down-at-heels fishing vessels now use it, is the first known seaport. From here the Phoenicians spread out to conquer the Mediterranean. They were the most intrepid seafarers, for they were the first to entrust themselves to the high seas.

Why so much began here on this little point of land under the shadow of the Lebanon mountains is something of a mystery. Byblos, now called Jebail, wears its old age lightly, and but for its ruins might be any obscure village on any Mediterranean coast. Here history and even prehistory lie spread out under the sun. You can walk down to the sea and find half-buried in a hollow a broken egg-shaped jar which still contains the bones of a Chalcolithic man. He lies there in a foetal position, and near his shoulder there is an earthenware pot once filled with grain to support him in the afterlife; jewelry was placed beside him so that he could adorn himself when he awakened; and there were stone maceheads and bronze weapons so that he could fight again. More than fourteen hundred of these eggs have been discovered. Nothing quite like them has been found elsewhere.

I came to Byblos on a hot and sultry day, sometimes clouded over, and sometimes through the torn clouds the sun flashed on the sea. I wandered among the thistles from one Chalcolithic grave to another, marveling over those broken egg-shells, while the sunlight played eerily, throwing shadows over them. It was strange that they were the only men who believed that a new life beckoned to them beyond the egg-shell, and stranger still that, while assuming the foetal position, they were armed and jeweled like grown men. They had evidently thought out a cosmology, and perhaps their gods were the small obelisks that lay nearby. They were roughly hewn, two or three feet high, unimpressive in our eyes, one obelisk standing beside another, forming a stone forest. I thought of Dushara, the god of the mountains at Petra, who was also worshiped in the form of an obelisk, and of the ancient Semitic adoration of rocks and mountain tops, and wondered whether the obelisks were not representations of holy mountains. They huddled together, leaned on one another, were of different heights and textures, could be explained in a hundred different ways, none of them satisfactory.

On a small space of about twelve acres we can trace the life of Byblos over seven thousand years.

There, lying in the open, are the Chalcolithic graves and the obelisks beneath the ancient walls, which were rebuilt every two hundred years or so over a period of 1,500 years. At first they were fishermen rather than seamen; they did not venture far beyond their bays and inlets. Gradually there comes evidence of wider explorations. At the beginning of the second millennium B.C. they encountered the Egyptians, who prized the wood that grew all over Lebanon, and Byblos became the chief center for the export of timber to the Egyptian empire. From this trade came power, wealth and influence. Byblos imported papyrus from Egypt and in turn exported it to Greece and the islands, and the Greek word *biblia,* meaning bundles of papyrus from Byblos, came to mean "book," and hence the word "bible." Inevitably the Egyptians conquered the Levant, inevitably there were uprisings, and the conquest began all over again. The evidence of the Egyptian presence in Byblos is found in the innumerable scarabs, seals, jars and statues which betray their Egyptian origin, all discovered on that little spit of land overlooking the Mediterranean. But there is also evidence of the Byblian influence on Egypt, for the Semitic god Adonis born in the mountains above Byblos subtly influenced the cult of Osiris. Byblos became a religious center celebrated for its vast temples, its priestesses and its hymns. About 500 B.C. the Byblians, Tyrians and Sidonians began to build their empire overseas. They colonized Carthage in North Africa and New Carthage in Spain; they held command of the seas until it was wrested from them by the Romans. Carthage perished, New Carthage became a Roman colony, and Byblos remained an important port. The Byzantines held it, and then the Crusaders came and built a fortress and a church which still remain; and then came the Turks, and then the French, and the British captured it at the end of World War I. The tides of empire were flung against this shining coast, and died away. Today there is only a small huddled village with too many gas stations and too many Coca-Cola stands.

I spent a day wandering among the wild thistles of those twelve acres which have witnessed the rise and fall of seventeen empires. Nebuchadnezzar came, and Assurbanipal, and Ramses II, and a hundred others. They burned and tortured, and carved statues of themselves and wrote their names on the rocks of the Dog River nearby to celebrate their magnificence, and it came to nothing, or very little. Byblos was the New York of its day, and I wondered what New York would look like in three thousand years. There was silence in my twelve acres of ruins, and the most living thing was a skeleton curled up in a broken egg, until a small child came whimpering among the thistles and his mother came running up to find him. The bright blue sea was empty until a small fishingboat put out silently to sea.

INDEX

	DATE DUE		

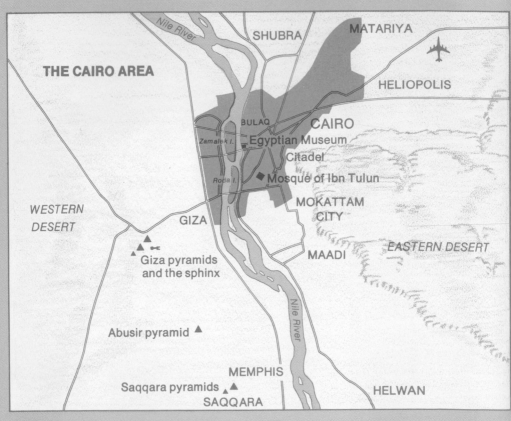

THE CAIRO AREA

SHUBRA

MATARIYA

HELIOPOLIS

Nile River

BULAQ

CAIRO

Zamalek I.

Egyptian Museum

Citadel

Roda I.

Mosque of Ibn Tulun

WESTERN
DESERT

GIZA

MOKATTAM
CITY

MAADI

EASTERN DESERT

▲
▲ Giza pyramids
and the sphinx

Nile River

Abusir pyramid ▲

MEMPHIS

Saqqara pyramids ▲▲

HELWAN

SAQQARA

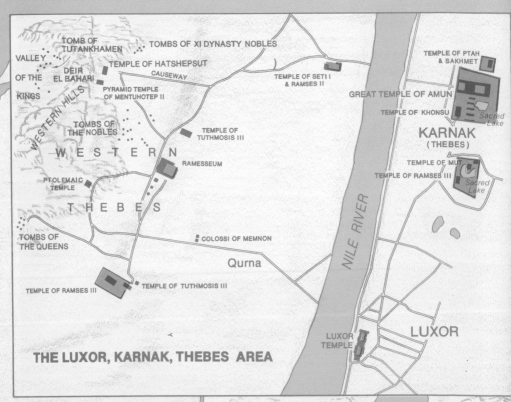

TOMB OF
TUTANKHAMEN

TOMBS OF XI DYNASTY NOBLES

TEMPLE OF PTAH
& SAKHMET

VALLEY
OF THE
KINGS

DEIR
EL BAHARI

TEMPLE OF HATSHEPSUT

CAUSEWAY

TEMPLE OF SETI I
& RAMSES II

GREAT TEMPLE OF AMUN

PYRAMID TEMPLE
OF MENTUHOTEP II

TEMPLE OF KHONSU

Sacred
Lake

WESTERN HILLS

TOMBS OF
THE NOBLES

W E S T E R N

TEMPLE OF
TUTHMOSIS III

KARNAK
(THEBES)

TEMPLE OF MUT

TEMPLE OF RAMSES III

RAMESSEUM

Sacred
Lake

PTOLEMAIC
TEMPLE

T H E B E S

NILE RIVER

TOMBS OF
THE QUEENS

COLOSSI OF MEMNON

Qurna

TEMPLE OF RAMSES III

TEMPLE OF TUTHMOSIS III

LUXOR

LUXOR
TEMPLE

THE LUXOR, KARNAK, THEBES AREA

Nile R.

GULF OF
SUEZ